MW00827280

KIDS EXPLORE
CHICAGO

Other books in the series

Kids Explore Boston
Kids Explore Florida

KIDS EXPLORE

CHICAGO

Susan D. Moffat

**Includes:
Art Institute of Chicago,
The Power House,
Shedd Aquarium,
Wacky Pirate Cruise,
and much more**

ADAMS PUBLISHING
Holbrook, Massachusetts

Copyright ©1995, Adams Media Corporation. All rights reserved.
This book, or parts thereof, may not be reproduced in any form
without permission from the publisher; exceptions are made for
brief excerpts used in published reviews.

Published by Adams Media Corporation
260 Center Street, Holbrook, MA 02343

ISBN: 1-55850-499-0

Printed in Korea.

J   I   H   G   F   E   D   C   B   A

Library of Congress Cataloging-in-Publication Data
Moffat, Susan D.
Kids explore Chicago : the very best kids' activities within an easy drive of Chicago / Susan D.
Moffat
    p.   cm.
    Includes index.
    ISBN: 1-55850-499-0
    1. Chicago (Ill.)—Guidebooks. 2. Chicago Region (Ill.)—Guidebooks. 3. Family
recreation—Illinois—Chicago—Guidebooks. 4. Family recreation—Illinois—Chicago Region—
Guidebooks. 5. Children—Travel—Illinois—Chicago—Guidebooks. 6. Children—Travel—
Illinois—Chicago Region—Guidebooks. I. Title.
F548.18.M64   1995
917.73'110443'083—dc20   94-47329
                                                   CIP

This publication is designed to provide accurate and authoritative information with regard to the
subject matter covered. It is sold with the understanding that the publisher is not engaged in
rendering legal, accounting, or other professional advice. If legal advice or other expert assistance
is required, the services of a competent professional person should be sought.
               — From a *Declaration of Principles* jointly adopted by a Committee of the American Bar
                          Association and a Committee of Publishers and Associations

Cover design: Peter Gouck
Front cover and interior photos: Susan D. Moffat (except where noted)
Rear cover photo: Laif Reid

This book is available at quantity discounts for bulk purchases.
For information, call 1-800-872-5627.

For busy parents who are committed to spending quality time with their children

ACKNOWLEDGMENTS

Thanks go out to the many people who have helped me along the way–the public relations departments and directors of the sites; Sam Moffat Agoos for being such a ham; Joe Delinks, even though he stuck his tongue out way too many times; the DeGroot family for offering shelter; Hoppy and Allison Snowden for being part of my family *and* living outside of Chicago; Rick Dey for his editing and commitment to the series; Peter Gouck for putting it all together; Stefan Pagacik for his baseball expertise; Denny Williams, who cared for Aki; Tory Broadus for her flute and smile; Bob Lacey for constant support; and Ivette, Adrian, and Luis Candela for *ayudandome* in many ways.

TABLE OF CONTENTS

INTRODUCTION

When I first thought about doing the Chicago book for my Kids Explore series, I had visions of gang wars and thermometers registering zero, and the term "windy city" sent shivers deep in my bones. Although there is a breeze that sweeps through the city (and sometimes almost *throws* you against the buildings), I learned that the term "windy city" derives not from whipping winds and frigid winter temperatures, but from politicians known for boasting and long-windedness in the late nineteenth century. I also found that, as in any city, there are areas to stay away from but, if you're careful, you'll be generally safe.

I never expected a city in the middle of America to offer such diversity for kids. Chicago is loaded with culture and history in its museums, art galleries, architecture, zoos, and public displays. It also has twenty-six miles of sandy beaches and parks that stretch along Lake Michigan, and every square inch contains a possibility for exploration. A city of contrasts, Chicago has an eclectic mix of cultures, a mishmash of architectural styles, and an extreme range of temperatures.

When visiting the city's larger attractions, don't try to see too much in one day. At each site grab a brochure, sit down, and choose the attractions which most interest you. Otherwise, trying to "see it all," you'll become tired, frustrated and angry (*grrr*). Also, try working ice cream, lunch, Frisbee, meditation, or whatever your thing is into your day.

Chicago has an impressive mass transportation system of buses, trains, and subways that will take you almost anywhere in the city. One *cool tip*, which will make your life easier, is that the Chicago Transportation Authority, or "CTA" as it's known, will, at any time you call (312/836-7000), provide directions. A patient voice tells you which bus, train, or subway to take, and offers time schedules. (This was an absolute lifesaver for me!) A good way to find the sites around downtown Chicago is to look at **Directions** under each site in this book and find the area listing (i.e., Loop Area or Grant Park), then locate your destination on the map at the back of this guide.

Two valuable sources of information to call before venturing into the city are the Illinois Travel Center at 800/223-0121 and the Chicago Travel Center at 800/487-2446. Ask for a free travel packet that includes maps, calendars, and guides. And keeping in mind that times, exhibits, special programs, and prices change on a regular basis, it is a good idea to call any site first for current information.

Putting this book together has been a true adventure. I hope you and the kids enjoy exploring Chicago as much as I did. Happy exploration!

—Susan D. Moffat

FUN SCALE

The balloon ratings are the result of asking a number of questions, including: How long will the attraction hold a child's attention? Does it have educational value? Will it make the children smile or laugh? Is it interactive and hands-on? Is the price of admission fair? Are the facilities safe, well maintained, and appropriately supervised? Is it a site where both parents and children can find interest and have fun?

I would like to stress that sites with only one- or two-balloon ratings are worth visiting, or they wouldn't be reviewed here; however, only those which score highest in the areas of consideration are five-ballooners!

 One balloon—Not worth any extra energy to get there; but, if you do happen to be in the neighborhood, you might take a gander.

 Two balloons—Not the most fun place on the planet for kids, but it has some redeeming qualities.

 Three balloons—A middle-of-the-road site on the fun scale, and worth a visit.

 **Four balloons**—Great place, and well worth a visit.

 **Five balloons**—Holy cow! The ultimate in fun and definitely not to be missed.

ICON EXPLANATION

Wheelchair Accessible   **Restaurant**   **Picnicking**   **Rest Rooms**   **Gift Shop**

"BEST OF" RATINGS

(These sites are "best of" for all ages, unless otherwise noted.)

Adler Planetarium
Art Institute of Chicago
Brookfield Zoo
Chicago by Air—"Learn to Fly before
      You Drive" (5 and up)
Field Museum of Natural History
Indiana Dunes
Kohl Children's Museum (2-10)
Lincoln Park Zoo
Museum of Science and Industry
Power House (8 and up)
Shedd Aquarium
Wacky Pirate Cruise (2-10)

FIELD MUSEUM OF NATURAL HISTORY
Roosevelt Road at Lakeshore Drive
Chicago, IL 60605
(312) 922-9410

FUN SCALE

Say hello to the world's largest mounted dinosaur as she greets you at the door. Look up at the four-story tall skeleton of a Brachiosaurus. The enormous terrestrial beast weighed about eighty-five tons in the flesh, and was forty-feet tall and seventy-five feet long. (Holy dinosaurs!) Continue on your journey inside the Field Museum of Natural History, which has an extensive permanent collection with dynamic changing exhibits. Ten acres of anthropology, botany, geology, and zoology are waiting for you to explore.

Learn about the mysterious world of the ancient Egyptians. Step into **Inside Ancient Egypt** and a life-size mastaba tomb. Look around at the twenty-three mummies. Some of their faces

are painted green for protection, rumor has it, against the night demons. Lift water from the Nile River with a simple lever device. Try a hand at pulling a three-ton stone block as the pyramid builders did. Check out the Egyptian marketplace.

Moving along to another area of the world, why not sample Polynesia? **Traveling the Pacific** is a permanent exhibit that exposes visitors to the wonders of the south seas through dramatic recreations and artifacts of the islands. See glowing lava. Walk on a windswept beach and listen to the sounds of the surf. Learn why some canoes have sails. Check out the Tahitian marketplace and experience life in a traditional village.

Experience a true sense of diversity on another continent with a visit to **Africa**. Travel back and forth through time and space in a variety of exhibits. Listen to music on computers. Learn about food preparation. See ivory tusks that tell a story. From mountaintop to desert, the terrain varies and so does the clothing. See examples of desert clothing–the key to coolness is found in covering up with heavy wrap-arounds. Push the button and listen to the Tuareg camel song.

Yank, push, slide, and pull your way through **DNA to Dinosaurs**. The spectacular exhibit explores the history and evolution of life on Earth–from the earliest single-celled DNA-based form of life through those in the Age of Dinosaurs. Time is a difficult concept to grasp. Turn the crank on the register to calculate years: How far are we today from the time of the dinosaurs? Push the button to find out.

"Psst over here!" I heard a voice, and turned to follow the light and sound for one explanation of how life began. Here, you can play with beaded strings and turn canvas bags inside out to learn about cloning and mutations or make a fossil rubbing. Computer games teach about extinction and an accordion-like button will activate dinosaur voices.

Many other exhibits inhabit the museum including **Sizes**, where you can find the real meaning of big and little; **The Place for Wonder**, an exhibit of many touchables from toys of foreign peoples to woolly mammoth teeth; and **Plants of the World**, a space filled with flora from algae to orchids.

Age Range: Any age. **Hours:** 9:00 A.M. to 5:00 P.M. daily. Closed Christmas, New Years, and Thanksgiving. **Admission:** *Field Museum only*–Adults $5.00; children (3-17), seniors or students with ID $3.00. *Special Family Rate*–maximum $16.00. *DNA to Dinosaurs only*–Adults $2.00; children (3-17), seniors, or students with ID $1.00. Wednesdays, excluding **DNA to Dinosaurs,** are free. **Time Allowance:** 2 to 4 hours. **Directions:** Grant Park. **Parking:** Pay-lots. **Wheelchair Accessible:** Yes. Wheelchair and stroller rentals available. **Restaurant:** Yes. **Picnicking:** Yes. **Rest Rooms:** Yes, with changing tables. **Gift Shop:** Yes; fossils, plastic dinos, T-shirts.

13

ADLER PLANETARIUM
1300 South Lake Shore Drive
Chicago, IL 60605
(312) 322-0300

Ever wonder if we're alone in the Universe? Learn more about outerspace at the Adler Planetarium. Explore three floors of activities that deal in astronomy and space exploration, and feature telescopes, planet models, and space transporters. Then, traveling on an escalator, transport yourself to the Sky Theater.

Begin your planetarium journey on the first floor with a hands-on exploration of the planets. Spin the **Moon Shadows** wheel and see the phases of the earth's moon. Step on the footprints of **Jupiter Trip** and travel to that planet. If you're weight-watching, you might decide to skip the trip to Jupiter, because you would weigh much more there than here; on the other hand, on the **Moon Trip** you'll weigh less–but don't be caught there in the daylight: The temperature is hot enough to boil water. (Yikes!) If you're planning a trip to the **Sun**, proceed with caution. You'll catch on fire in a millisecond. Check out the real moon rock and meteorite. Learn how to use a **Star Finder**. Hold it up and view the heavenly bodies that dot the sky at night.

On the second floor, in **Seeing the Universe**, learn about the early telescope discoveries of outer space. Step into the **Hall of Telescopes** and see models dating as far back as Galileo's day. Now's the chance to use a telescope and find your favorite star.

14

© Copyright K. Cooper

Travel from our planet Earth to outer space. Hop on the *steep* escalator and travel through a space that's surrounded by stars and darkness as you're whisked up to **Sky Theater**. Relax in the comfy chairs and experience a multi-image show that will answer some of those lingering, extra-terrestrial questions and provoke others. Some shows are viewed with 3-D glasses and have the effect of being "in your face" and very real. See a close-up view of the moon, a star being born, or a volcano erupting on Venus.

Special **Sky Shows** for pre-schoolers and parents bring you face to face with characters like Meteor Mouse and Cosmic Cat who are trying to solve the puzzles of the universe in their star-filled adventures. Learn the difference between a planet and a star as you identify famous constellations such as the

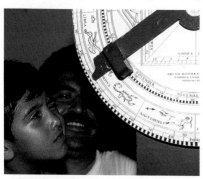

Big Dipper and Orion's Belt. The semi-animated shows last forty-five minutes, and are sure to provoke those hard-to-answer questions from the kids.

Don't forget to look at the bronze sundial which was sculpted by Henry Moore. It's outside, in front of the planetarium, and it really tells time–without batteries!

Age Range: Other than the Saturday and Sunday morning Sky Shows for pre-schoolers, the Planetarium is fun for ages 6 and up. **Hours:** 9:00 A.M. to 5:00 P.M., daily; 9:00 A.M. to 9:00 P.M., Friday. **Admission:** Adults $4.00, children (17 and under) and seniors (65 and over) $2.00. Tuesday free. **Time Allowance:** 1 1/2 to 2 hours. **Directions:** Grant Park. **Parking:** Meters and pay-lots. **Wheelchair Accessible:** Yes. **Restaurant:** Cafeteria only. **Picnicking:** Yes. **Rest Rooms:** Yes, with changing tables. **Gift Shop:** Yes; prisms, space jackets, planet mugs.

CHICAGO BY AIR
"LEARN TO FLY BEFORE YOU DRIVE"
P.O. Box 16634
Meigs Field
Chicago, IL 16634
(708) 524-1172

FUN SCALE 🎈🎈🎈🎈🎈

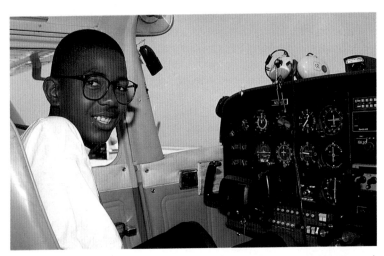

"The mixture goes rich. The master switch on," says the control pilot. And then you're off–flying above the Adler Planetarium, soaring along side the Sears Tower (yikes!), zipping down Lakeshore Drive, and finally landing safely back on Meigs Field runway.

If your child has ever dreamt of becoming a pilot or flying a plane, now's his or her chance. "Kids Can Fly before They Drive" offers an airborne trip with a certified flight instructor and an experience behind the control-wheel of a four-seater Cessna 172. Your child actually sits in the driver's seat and

operates the controls. (Don't worry, the instructor has the main-overriding controls.)

The flight begins with brief instructions by the pilot. Check the fuel level. Inspect the vertical and air speed dials. The steering is done with your feet when on the runway–use the top of the pedal for brakes and the bottom to steer. The left-and-right steering, and up-and-down motions, are regulated by the control-wheel while in the air. The instructors are extremely patient and willing to answer any questions.

Your child should not expect to return home, ready for his or her own airplane. However, the young pilot will have had an experience of a lifetime, and possibly have fulfilled a dream. Call for reservations.

Age Range: 5 and up. **Hours:** 6:00 A.M. to 9:00 P.M. daily, weather permitting. **Admission:** $125.00 for two, $15.00 for a third person (three-passenger limit). **Time Allowance:** 30 minutes. **Directions:** Meigs Field. **Parking:** Free lots. **Wheelchair Accessible:** No. **Restaurant:** Snackbar only. **Picnicking:** No, but nearby. **Rest Rooms:** Yes. **Gift Shop:** No.

JOHN G. SHEDD AQUARIUM
1200 South Lake Shore Drive
Chicago, IL 60605
(312) 939-2426

FUN SCALE

Electric eels glide sleekly through the water. Penguins occasionally waddle over to the edge and dive in. Hungry piranhas shred small prey to bones in seconds. Nurse sharks lie for hours on shallow, sunlit ocean floors. So goes a typical day at the Shedd Aquarium.

With 70 percent of our planet occupied by water, and 97 percent of that by salt water, shouldn't we learn as much as we can about the creatures which inhabit those waters? This is a good place to start.

A likely spot to begin is outside the gigantic, glass enclosed 900,000-gallon tank housing the **Tropical Coral Reef**. More than 350 types of Caribbean fish constantly glide around and dart in and out of the reef. Divers hand-feed the fish several times a day. Did you know

© Copyright John G. Shedd Aquarium

the six-foot moray eel's green body is actually blue with a coat of thick yellow mucus that protects the skin from abrasions and makes the color *appear* green? Watch damselfish with bright yellow tails and blue freckles duck behind the corals when in danger.

While you're circling around the central tank, you can also see iguanas in **Animals of the Caribbean** exhibit. Do you know that males are brown and as long as three feet, while females are green and typically eighteen inches long? They establish territorial rights by quickly bobbing their heads.

Check out the flashlight fish in **Animals of Indo-Pacific**. They're tiny deep-water fish that zip around and confuse their predators by blinking their spooky headlights.

Admire the colorful anemones in **Animals of Cold Oceans** as they seem to wave hello in the water. They may look like a harmless flower but, in reality, they use their venomous tentacles to obtain food. See humongous

18

North American lobsters that can grow to weigh up to fifty pounds. (Holy lobsters!)

The **Animals of the Great Lake Region** is home to river otters. These cute creatures, which flop awkwardly around on land, swim gracefully through the water. They're *very* busy!

In **Freshwater Animals of the Americas**, don't expect to see much action from the alligator snapping turtles. If you're lucky, they will surface for air about once an hour. Electric eels, on the other hand, zap their prey with a powerful electrical charge frequently.

If you're able to visit the **Oceanarium**, it will be well worth the extra dollars spent. The tickets are "timed," meaning that you may only enter during the time printed on your ticket. Once in, however, you may stay as long as you like.

The **Oceanarium** recreates the ecosystem of the Pacific Northwest coast in its full glory and is the largest indoor marine mammal pavilion in the world. Begin with an exploration of its nature trail. Bird songs fill the air as you walk through the lush, temperate rainforest. Sea otters busily explore their own marine environment. Observe–but don't touch–in the shallows of the tide pool fuzzy white anemones, crabs, sea stars, and mussels existing side by side. The simulated island, volcanic dike, glacial grooves, and a barren rock demonstrate the results of nature's awesome forces.

Five *Marine Mammal Presentations* happen daily. White-sided dolphins

© Copyright John G. Shedd Aquarium

do spectacular double flips in the air, breech in the water, and make sounds through a blow-hole in their head. Beluga whales, who use what we would call sonar to locate objects in the water, also "spy-hop"–a maneuver by which the whale, treading water, with its tail, raises its head out of the water to see the world above sea level. Beluga whales have been nicknamed "sea canaries" because their vocals sound like bird calls.

The *Underwater Viewing Gallery* allows a different perspective. Come eye-to-eye with the creatures as they go about their daily business. How long can whales and dolphins stay underwater before coming up for air?

Located above the amphitheater is the *Penguin Shore* where a large colony of penguins lives. These aquatic birds can't fly, but *can* swim–up to twenty-five miles per hour.

Age Range: Any age. **Hours:** 9:00 A.M. to 6:00 P.M. daily. Closed Christmas and New Year's Day. "Timed tickets" are issued for the Oceanarium. The time printed on the ticket is the time the ticket holder may enter. Scheduled educational presentations in the Oceanarium take place at 10:30 A.M., 12 noon, and at 1:30, 3:00, and 4:00 P.M. **Admission:** *Aquarium and Oceanarium*–Adults (12-64) $8.00 ($4.00*), seniors (65 and over) and children (3-11) $6.00 ($3.00*). *Aquarium only*–Adults $4.00, seniors and children $3.00. * Visits to the *original* Aquarium building are free on Thursdays. Asterisked rates denote admission to the Oceanarium on Thursdays only. **Time Allowance:** 2 hours to full-day. **Directions:** Grant Park. **Parking:** Pay-lots and short-term meters. **Wheelchair Accessible:** Yes. Wheelchairs loaners are available. Strollers are not permitted in the Oceanarium. Stroller check is available. **Restaurant:** Yes, and a snackbar. **Picnicking:** No. **Rest Rooms:** Yes, with changing tables. **Gift Shop:** Yes; stuffed manatees, rubber fish, sweatshirts. *Cool Tip:* Tickets should be purchased in advance during the summer and can be purchased from Ticketmaster (312) 902-1500. *Cool Tip #2:* If you plan to go into the Oceanarium, take a sweater. Even in the summer, it can be chilly.

CONCERTS FOR KIDS, TOO!
Grant Park Concert Society
P.O. Box 94291
Chicago, IL 60690
(800) 588-4443 or (312) 819-0614

FUN SCALE

© Copyright Grant Park Concert Society

Add Concerts For Kids, Too! to your list of Chicago freebies. Ten summer concerts in Grant Park, with compositions ranging from symphonies to ballet and Broadway scores, allow for exposure to something that often seems more for grown ups. Turn the kids on to the delights of classical music and theater. Performances are done in a kid-friendly manner and are often performed by young people. Call for more information.

Age Range: Kids will listen to music and watch dance and theater for varying amounts of time, depending on age and sophistication. **Hours:** Late June through August. Hours vary. **Admission:** Free. **Time Allowance:** 1 to 2 hours. **Directions:** Grant Park. **Parking:** Pay garages in the park. **Wheelchair Accessible:** Yes. **Restaurant:** No. **Picnicking:** Yes. **Rest Rooms:** Yes. **Gift Shop:** No.

THE ART INSTITUTE OF CHICAGO
111 South Michigan Avenue
Chicago, IL 60603-6110
(312) 443-3500

FUN SCALE

If you can peel the kids away from crawling on the six thousand-pound bronze lions that guard the entrance, a visit *inside* the museum will be almost as much fun for them. The huge, impressive space, subdivided into galleries, is filled with glorious art, from Classical Greek to contemporary American. You're more than likely to get lost whether you have a map or not, but don't forget to pick one up at the entrance–it could help you find the bathrooms.

Kids will want to head straight for the **Kraft General Foods Education Center** and launch into an exploration of the world of art at a kid-level. See twelve works of art from the African, ancient American, European, and twentieth-century museum collections, and get to know them through games, interactive computers, and music. It's a simplified, hands-on, fun way to learn about the techniques and concepts of art.

Step into the cozy *Family Room* and put together a puzzle, play an art game, or listen to a story. A short video in the lobby describes how exhibits are

put together and maintained. In *Gallery 16*, you'll find original illustrations of children's books, which change every three months.

Invest in a *Family Self-Guide* (they're only 25¢) and explore the rest of the museum. The guide is a kind of a treasure hunt that gives you cool hints and leads you through the museum in pursuit of masterpieces. For instance, does a painting of a farm couple standing in a field and resting on a pitchfork ring a bell? You may have seen another version of it on a box of Cornflakes. Head to the **Modern Art Gallery** to find the famous painting, "American Gothic," by Grant Wood.

The Art Institute has one of the world's largest collections of impressionist paintings. Head for the **Impressionism and Post-Impressionism Gallery** and check out the paintings that are made totally of dots. It's a technique called pointillism, and kids can easily relate to it; you can find excellent examples in the work of Georges Seurat.

In the **Thorne Miniature Rooms** stoop and peek into the tiny spaces. There are sixty-eight fully-furnished rooms fully decorated with American and European furnishings, right down to napkins on the tables and chandeliers hung from ceilings.

And while absorbed by smallness, you might step into the **Arthur Rubloff Paperweight Collection**. Imagine–a collection devoted solely to paperweights! The wildly-intricate details in glass that is designed to keep paper from blowing away are, along with their attention to shape and texture, what make paperweights an art form.

Fans of Medieval times shouldn't miss the **George F. Harding Arms and Armor Collection**. This impressive reserve dominates Gunsaulus Hall and is full of knightless shining armor and imposing arms, including swords,

crossbows, and arrows. At the end of the long hall, sit down and gaze at "The American Window," a beautiful stained glass work by Marc Chagall. What do you think might be happening in the window scene?

Check out the awesome twelfth-century Buddhas in the **Indian and Southeastern Asian Gallery**. They're made of limestone and weigh up to three thousand pounds. How did they ever get them to Chicago?

The Institute offers a variety of programs for families which include *Family Gallery Walks*. The walks are designed for people nine years and up, and each week explore a different theme designed to launch kids and parents into the museum's changing collections. They take place on Saturdays from October through June and last for about one hour. The summer schedule is limited. Call for exact times.

Age Range: The Kraft Center is targeted for kids 7 through 12, but younger children will enjoy certain sections of the museum for varying amounts of time. **Hours:** Monday, Wednesday, Thursday, and Friday 10:30 A.M. to 4:30 P.M.; Tuesday 10:30 A.M. to 8:00 P.M.; Saturday 10:00 A.M. to 5:00 P.M.; Sundays and holidays 12 noon to 5:00 P.M. Open daily except Christmas and Thanksgiving. **Admission:** Tuesdays are free. On other days visitors pay what they wish but must pay something. Recommended fee is adults $6.50; seniors, children (6 and up), and students with ID $3.25. **Time Allowance:** 2 to 4 hours. **Directions:** Grant Park. **Parking:** Pay-lots. **Wheelchair Accessible:** Yes, Columbus Drive entrance only. A limited number of wheelchairs and strollers are available free of charge. **Restaurant:** Yes, from fine dining to cafeteria. **Picnicking:** Yes, in the Museum Gardens. **Rest Rooms:** Yes, some with changing tables. **Gift Shop:** Yes; art games, umbrellas, blow-up mummies.

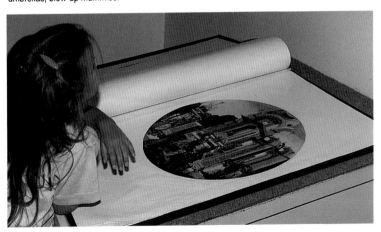

CHICAGO CULTURAL CENTER
78 East Washington Street
Chicago, IL 60602
(312) 744-2400 or (800) 487-2446

FUN SCALE

Perhaps a perfect first stop, the **Chicago Office of Tourism Visitor Information Center**, located in the Chicago Cultural Center, is loaded with information about current happenings in Chicagoland. There are all sorts of free events happening throughout the Center. A seven-minute, multi-lingual video called *Round the Loop* serves as a solid orientation to the city. After picking up pamphlets, schedules, brochures, maps, and anything else of interest, hook up with a free tour of the building. (It's not *absolutely* necessary, you can take a self-guided tour, but you'll learn some intriguing facts about the history of the building.)

"Remarkable!" is a sentiment commonly expressed by visitors as they gaze at the architecture. Look for the repeating natural shapes and patterns: Pinecones, flowers, spider webs, and seashells are all discovered in the intricately-detailed structures. Stairs and walls are detailed with marble and colorful mosaics made of thousands of tiny pieces of stone, seashells, and glass. Look up at coffered ceilings made of zillions of boxes filled with mosaic tiles, and a dome made of Tiffany stained glass.

Free family programs, which change monthly and run throughout the year, include live performances of puppet shows and storytelling, and films. Call for more information.

Age Range: All ages, depending on performance. **Hours:** Building hours–Monday through Thursday 10:00 A.M. to 7:00 P.M.; Friday 10:00 A.M. to 6:00 P.M.; Saturday 10:00 A.M. to 5:00 P.M.; Sunday 12 noon to 5:00 P.M. Closed on holidays. **Admission:** Free. **Time Allowance:** Varies with performance. **Directions:** Loop area. **Parking:** Pay-lots and short-term meters. **Wheelchair Accessible:** Yes, through the 77 East Randolph Street entrance. **Restaurant:** Coffee bar only. **Picnicking:** No, but across the street. **Rest Rooms:** Yes, with changing tables. **Gift Shop:** Small, with pins, post cards, paper weights.

AMERICAN POLICE CENTER AND MUSEUM
1705-25 South State Street
Chicago, IL 60616
(312) 431-0005

FUN SCALE

"The prevention of crime is everyone's responsibility," and the American Police Center and Museum attempts to spread the word through eye-opening and sometimes-startling exhibits. Find out how a police station operates in the **Communication Section**. From a simple blow of a whistle or banging a night stick on the ground to the high-tech radios of today, communication is an important aspect of police work. Learn how an emergency call is handled.

The **Identification Display** gives a historical view of the evolution of an increasingly difficult task. From merely taking body measurements to fingerprinting in 1905 to DNA determination today, the methods are documented and explained in this exhibit.

The **Smuggling Display** reveals many of the ways illegal drugs are smuggled into this country, monitored by enforcement agencies, and—sometimes–confiscated. Canine units are trained to smell out the drugs; German shepherds and rottweilers are primarily used because they're alert,

potentially ferocious, and easily trained.

The **Drug Display** is one of the more disturbing exhibits. You'll see a coffin filled with actual drugs beneath a photo taken of a sixteen-year-old just before she died of an

26

overdose. The photograph is grueling and leaves a lasting impression.

Unless you're into gore, I would suggest passing by the **Crime Victim Pictures**. Horrifying images of violations against innocent people line the case and are startling, to say the least.

Gangster Alley provides a window into the Capone Era in Chicago. See Al "Scarface" Capone and other gangsters of the Prohibition Era as they're displayed, along with some of their weapons. Note the fingernail-scratch marks on the arms of the electric chair where those who weren't shot died.

Other than sitting in the electric chair or posing in Mugshot Alley, nothing here is hands-on. Several of the exhibits are upsetting–for any age. Unless parents are willing to explain some of the reasons behind certain exhibits, it could be a disturbing experience for kids.

Saturday group tours are available by calling in advance for a reservation.

Age Range: 2-5 no; 6-8 possibly, if with adults who are willing to explain some of the exhibits; 9 and up probably. **Hours:** 9:00 A.M. to 4:30 P.M. daily. **Admission:** Suggested donation of adults $3.00, seniors $2.00, children (under 12) $1.50. **Time Allowance:** 30 minutes. **Directions:** South of the Loop. **Parking:** Free-lot. **Wheelchair Accessible:** Yes. **Restaurant:** No. **Picnicking:** No. **Rest Rooms:** Yes. **Gift Shop:** Yes; plastic guns, police sirens with batteries, T-shirts.

GALLERY 37
on State Street between
Randolph and Washington Streets
(312) 744-1424

FUN SCALE

Gallery 37 is an award-winning arts program which employs hundreds of selected high school youths each summer. The valuable program is funded by the city of Chicago and teens apprentice under professional artists and are actually *paid* to learn and create art.

The public is invited to walk from tent to tent and watch as young artists create magnificent murals, furniture, jewelry, architectural models, ceramics, paintings, and music. Catch an occasional live performance–music, poetry readings, dance, and short stories. Purchase a finished product in the **Retail Tent**. All proceeds from sales go back into the program.

In the **Outreach Tent**, under the

28

instruction of professional and apprentice artists, anyone of any age can create their own artwork. From paper making to jewelry to monoprints, let your imagination go wild. Take it home afterwards. Do you have a special wish? You're not alone. Write it down and add it to the always-growing **Chicago Wish-Line**, a clothesline sculpture which illustrates the wishes and dreams of Chicagoans and visitors to the city.

Free **Saturday Art Classes** are offered by teachers from the Art Institute of Chicago. Anyone, from neophyte to expert, can create art by printmaking, fabric painting, papermaking, figure drawing, or doing watercolors and take it home.

Age Range: *Gallery 37*–youths (14-20). *Outreach Tent* and *Saturday Art Classes*–all ages. **Hours:** *Outreach Tent*–Monday through Friday 10:00 A.M. to 4:00 P.M. *Art Classes*–Saturday 10:00 A.M. to 4:00 P.M. From early July to late August. No reservations necessary for either program. **Admission:** Free. **Time Allowance:** 30 minutes to stroll through, 2 hours to participate. **Directions:** Loop area. **Parking:** Pay-lots and short-term meters. **Wheelchair Accessible:** Yes. **Restaurant:** No, but nearby. **Picnicking:** Yes. **Rest Rooms:** Yes. **Gift Shop:** Yes; hand-made boxes, mirrors, jewelry.

"SKATE ON STATE" ICE RINK
On State Street between Washington and Randolph Streets
(312)744-3315

FUN SCALE

When the weather gets chilly, and the water freezes over, Block 37 turns into an ice skating rink. Lace up your skates, shove off, and skate awhile. This is another freebie sponsored by the Chicago Cultural Center.

© Copyright Willy Schmidt

Age Range: Any age. **Hours:** 9:00 A.M. to 7:30 P.M. daily, from the first weekend after Thanksgiving through February (weather permitting). **Admission:** Free. Skate rentals $2.00. **Time Allowance:** Varies. **Directions:** Loop area. **Parking:** Pay-lots and short-term meters. **Wheelchair Accessible:** Yes. **Restaurant:** No, but nearby. **Picnicking:** Yes. **Rest Rooms:** Yes. **Gift Shop:** No.

MUSEUM OF CONTEMPORARY PHOTOGRAPHY
600 South Michigan Avenue
Chicago, IL 60605
(312) 663-5554

FUN SCALE

© Copyright Thomas Nowak

Shutterbugs unite! Where else can you find such a wide range of photographically-related images, objects, and ideas? The Museum of Contemporary Photography is the only museum in the Midwest committed solely to exhibiting photographic images as an art form.

The main gallery holds exhibits which change five times a year. These contain provocative and innovative displays often going beyond what's considered typical photography and stretching the imagination.

Upstairs is the permanent collection of photographs produced after 1959. Rotating shows focus on American photography and feature work of such greats as Diane Arbus, Robert Frank, and Dorthea Lange.

Okay, there's nothing hands-on about the Museum of Contemporary Photography, and it's not exactly geared toward children, but why not expose the kids to the medium of photography as an art form? It may just spark their imagination in a positive way.

Age Range: 8 and up. **Hours:** 10:00 A.M. to 5:00 P.M. Monday, Tuesday, Wednesday, and Friday; 10:00 A.M. to 8:00 P.M. Thursday; 12 noon to 5:00 P.M. Saturday (closes at 4:00 P.M. daily in June and July). Closed Sunday, month of August, and holidays. **Admission:** Free. **Time Allowance:** About 30 minutes, varying with show. Call first to find what's being exhibited. **Directions:** Loop area. **Parking:** Pay-lots. **Wheelchair Accessible:** Yes. **Restaurant:** Snackbar only. **Picnicking:** No, but across the street. **Rest Rooms:** Yes. **Gift Shop:** No; only books affiliated with existing exhibit.

THOMAS HUGHES CHILDREN'S LIBRARY

The Chicago Public Library
Harold Washington Library Center
400 South State Street
Chicago, IL 60605
(312) 747-4200

FUN SCALE

Thomas Hughes, author of *Tom Brown's School Days*, organized a campaign in England to donate books to Chicago after the fire of 1871. Over eight thousand volumes were collected and shipped to the fire-ravaged city. (Kudos to Thomas Hughes!) This was the beginning of The Chicago Public Library as we know it today.

In 1991 the library moved from the site of the Chicago Cultural Center to a post-modern, classical-style building on South State Street. The grandiose granite-and-brick building is embellished with gargoyle-like owls (symbolizing wisdom) hanging at each corner, faces with puffed cheeks (representing the wind in the Windy City), and seed pods

in between (a reminder of the natural bounty of the Midwest).

The second floor is home to the Thomas Hughes Children's Library. Kid-size chairs, tables, art displays, and comfy-reading spaces make it a pleasant place to read in. Why not curl up to a good book in the **Storytelling Alcove**? The library holds about 100,000 volumes, including picture books, easy readers, fiction, reference materials, and science-project books. It is also home to **NatureConnections**, a special collection of natural history

objects that provide kids with an opportunity to learn about the environment.

Nearby, in the **Learning Center**, you can experiment with computers that are loaded with children's educational programs. Learn about the Aztec warriors or what happens when you mix yellow and blue. Staff members will also show you how to use a microcomputer. Kids love it! The Learning Center is only open at scheduled times, so call ahead.

To obtain a library card, a child must be a Chicago-area resident with a signature-

and-ID-providing parent; if you're not Chicago residents, you can spend time browsing. There's always something happening at the library. **Special Programs** include *Fabulous Fridays Children's Programs, Story Time Extravaganza, NatureConnections, craft events, magic and puppet shows,* and *family videos.* Call for specifics.

Age Range: 2 through 13. **Hours:** Monday 9:00 A.M. to 7:00 P.M.; Tuesday and Thursday 11:00 A.M. to 7:00 P.M.; Wednesday, Friday, and Saturday 9:00 A.M. to 5:00 P.M. Closed Sunday and holidays. **Admission:** Free. **Time Allowance:** 1 to 3 hours. **Directions:** Loop Area. **Parking:** Pay-lots. **Wheelchair Accessible:** Yes. **Restaurant:** Coffee shop only. **Picnicking:** No. **Rest Rooms:** Yes, with changing tables. **Gift Shop:** Yes; finger puppets, blow-up globes, books.

MUSEUM OF BROADCAST COMMUNICATIONS
Chicago Cultural Center
Michigan Avenue at Washington Street
Chicago, IL 60602-3407
(312) 629-6000

FUN SCALE

Couch potatoes unite! Step out and learn about what occupies a big chunk of many lives. Located in the landmark Chicago Cultural Center lies the Museum of Broadcast Communications, which examines contemporary American history solely through TV and radio.

In America's only **Radio Hall of Fame**, explore radio memorabilia back to the 1920s. Open Fibber McGee's closet and hear everything crash. See the original Mortimer Snerd and Charlie McCarthy puppets. Break into Jack Benny's vault, where the penny-pincher hoarded his wealth, and activate the alarm. See a variety of old radios; although you'll have to explain the significance to the kids, the exhibit's worth a peek.

The historical presentations in the **Television Exhibit Gallery** are always changing–from the first televised presidential debate between John Kennedy and Richard Nixon to Walt Disney clips.

In the **"One Minute Miracle,"** you'll find award-winning commercials from around the world. Choose from such greats as the one that first brought sneakers into popularity to the commercial that taught the world how to spell b-o-l-o-g-n-a.

The **Sportscaster's Cafe** brings great moments in sport's history to the screen. Pull up a chair and relive Michael Jordan slam-dunking his eight-zillionth basket or Mark Spitz swimming to his Olympic victory, to name only two.

News anchor wanna-bes, now's your chance. Clip on the fake shirt-front, pull on the blue blazer, and listen to instructions from the floor director. Lights, camera, action! You're reading the news from a video prompter and being recorded on tape. Who knows, a session in **Kraft's NewsCenter** may be the beginning of a career. Call (312) 629-6011 for reservations.

On the second floor you can catch-up on your favorite soaps, see Mickey Mouse Club classics, or listen to a radio broadcast. Sixty thousand hours of TV shows, commercials, and radio broadcasts, are accessible. Simply pay the $2.00 fee and choose from the zillions on the computer-retrieval system. Put on the headphones, relax in the comfy chairs, and imbibe. There's no time limit–you can vegetate for hours in the **Archives**!

Age Range: 7 and older. Kids should be able to read to participate in the Kraft TeleNewscenter. **Hours:** Monday through Saturday from 10:00 A.M. to 4:30 P.M., Sunday from 12 noon to 5:00 P.M. Closed all state and national holidays. Tours are conducted Monday through Friday at 10:30 A.M. and 2:30 P.M. and must be scheduled in advance by calling (312) 629-6017. **Admission:** Free admission to museum. Tour charge for all ages is $2.00 per person. $2.00 charge to access the archives. Kraft TeleNewsCenter tape costs $19.95. **Time Allowance:** 1/2 to 2 hours, or all day for major couch potatoes. The taping at the Kraft TeleNewsCenter takes 40 minutes per tape. **Directions:** Loop area. **Parking:** pay-lots and short-term meters. **Wheelchair Accessible:** Yes. Enter from the Randolph Street side. **Restaurant.** Coffee bar only. **Picnicking:** No. **Rest Rooms:** Yes, with changing tables. **Gift Shop:** Yes; Bozo the Clown noses, ventriloquist dummies, post cards.

35

SEARS TOWER SKYDECK
233 South Wacker Drive
Chicago, IL 60606
(312) 875-9696

FUN SCALE

Shoot straight up to the top of the world–via a high-speed elevator, and land on the 103rd floor of the Sears Tower.

But before you leave the lobby, see an eight-minute multimedia show that presents the colorful background of a multicultured city–Chicago. Then get set for some major ear-popping as you soar to the sky deck in under one minute.

Yawn a lot, exit the elevator, and ... You're at the top of the tallest office

building in the world. But is the structure secure? Yes: The Sears Tower is constructed of concrete and steel socketed into bedrock. And what about its 16,000 dirty windows? Don't worry: Six automatic washers clean them eight times a year.

Look all around. Chicago's eighty-seven neighborhoods stretch for twenty-five miles along Lake Michigan; consider that some fifty-four languages are spoken in them. Look eastward and out at the *Buckingham Fountain*. It was modeled after the ornate fountains of Versailles, in France. The fountain

splashes only from May through October and colored light shows illuminate the splashing daily from 9:00 to 11:00 P.M. And, if you look downward, you'll see the largest "moving mural" in the world. This orange kinetic mobile, "Universe," was created by Alexander Calder.

To the north you can see the *Merchandise Mart*, one of the largest commercial buildings in the world. Rumor has it, though, that the awesome art deco structure is about to be demolished. It rests at the edge of the Chicago River. According to early explorers of the 1600s, Native Americans had named the area *Chicagou*, meaning wild onion, due to the fact that it was swampy and had onions growing along the river's banks. Chicago was thus named after a wild onion. (Cool!)

In the west lie the complicated, spaghetti-like highways leading out to the suburbs. Look for the *United Center*, home court of the Bulls and rink of the Blackhawks.

Southward is *Comiskey Park*, home to the Chicago White Sox, *Adler Planetarium*, and *Shedd Aquarium*. On a clear day you can see Midway Airport.

Age Range: Any age. **Hours:** March through September 9:00 A.M. to 11:00 P.M. daily; October through February 10:00 A.M. to 10:00 P.M. daily. **Admission:** Adults $6.00, seniors $4.50, children (5-17) $3.25. Family rate $16.00–includes 2 adults and up to 6 children. **Time Allowance:** About an hour. **Directions:** Near North **Parking:** Pay lots. **Wheelchair Accessible:** Yes. **Restaurant:** Yes. **Picnicking:** No. **Rest Rooms:** Yes, with changing tables. **Gift Shop:** Yes; T-shirts, postcards, caps. *Cool Tip:* Lines are longest in the evenings and on weekend days. Why not take an early morning excursion and avoid the crowds?

THE ARTiFACT CENTER AT SPERTUS MUSEUM
Spertus Institute of Jewish Studies
618 South Michigan Avenue
Chicago, IL 60605
(312) 322-1754

FUN SCALE

Hey, could it be the missing link? You've taken out the pick and trowel and come across an old bone buried beneath a mound of sand. Dig on and discover other buried treasures–from ceramic shards to old coins.

The ARTiFACT Center, located in the basement of the Spertus Museum, provides hands-on archaeological experience. Young archaeologists go wild! Learn what an archaeologist does as you excavate the "**tel**," an area where, due to rich resources, many civilizations have lived over the years. The thirty-two foot long hill, divided into twelve sites, is planted with artifacts common to the ancient biblical world. Locate relics using the same techniques as archaeologists at a real site. Learn how to document your finds and guess their ages.

Step behind the scenes, into the **Tell Trail**, where you'll see a written description of what's in the trench. The date of the artifact and description of the people in power are revealed. How close were your guesses?

In the **Costume Quarter** try on old garments, step behind the podium, and speak to an audience of imaginary Israelites. Make jewelry in **Amulets and Ornaments**. Stamp a cuneiform sign in the clay tablet in **Writers Use Symbols**. Make a pot of terra cotta clay in the **Pottery Booth**. Build a simple musical instrument in the **Music Room**.

A favorite for kindergartners and younger kids is the **Israelite House**.

38

The space is perfect for digging around in a mini-sand pit, climbing on a wooden camel or lion, or dressing up in old clothes.

Further explorative possibilities involve touring the main part of the museum. It's a hands-off situation geared more toward adults, however. The extensive collection covers 3,500 years of Jewish history and portrays the Judaic life cycle from birth to death. Over three thousand artifacts fill the main gallery, including torah scrolls and an ornate torah ark built in 1913, Sabbath relics, amulets, and jewels.

The **Zell Holocaust Memorial** contains shocking photographs and artifacts. Videos show survivors sharing their feelings of loss and viewpoints of the Nazi atrocities. Although the exhibit is an important part of Judaic history and difficult to ignore, it is not meant to be the sole focus of the museum. You will have to decide whether your kids are old enough to absorb this twentieth-century horror.

Age Range: All ages. Preschoolers enjoy the Israeli Home. Older kids dig the ARTiFACT Center. **Hours:** Sunday through Thursday from 10:00 A.M. to 5:00 P.M. Group tours are available by appointment mornings and some afternoons. **Admission:** Adults $4.00; seniors, students, and children $2.00. Maximum family rate is $9.00. **Time Allowance:** About two hours. **Directions:** Loop area. **Parking:** Pay-lots. **Wheelchair Accessible:** Yes; even the trenches are the right height for wheelchairs. **Restaurant:** No, but nearby. **Picnicking:** No. **Rest Rooms:** Yes, with changing tables. **Gift Shop:** Yes.

"WACKY PIRATE CRUISE"
Mercury Skyline Cruiseline
Michigan Avenue and Wacker Drive
Chicago, IL
(312) 902-1500

FUN SCALE

Climb aboard the pirate ship with the flag displaying a skull and cross bones. Embark on a one-hour journey, lead by Buccaneer Bob. The adventure passes under the **Michigan Avenue Bridge**, goes by the **Water Arc**, which spits water for ten minutes every hour in celebration of the city's clean water (Kudos!), and then goes through the **Chicago River Lock**, which rises three-and-a-half feet to bring you to the level of **Lake Michigan**. After cruising near the **Navy Pier** and **Buckingham Fountain**, the ship returns home.

Buccaneer Bob explains the sites on his "pirate map" and leads kids in

sing-alongs and kazoo accompaniments as the boat motors along. Don't forget to say "Ahoy there!" when passing under a bridge! Young pirates receive a pirate hat, kazoo, and certificate stating that they've "survived" the cruise.

Age Range: 2-10. **Hours:** Thursday, Friday, Saturday, and Sunday mornings, from June 11 through September 4, at 10:00 A.M. **Admission:** Adults $7.50, children (11 and under) $5.00. **Time Allowance:** 1 hour. **Directions:** Loop area. **Parking:** Pay-lots. **Wheelchair Accessible:** No. **Restaurant:** No. **Picnicking:** Yes. **Rest Rooms:** Yes. **Gift Shop:** No.

"UNDER THE PICASSO"

Daley Civic Center
50 West Washington Street
Chicago, IL 60602
(312) F-I-N-E A-R-T (346-3278)

FUN SCALE

Why not bring your lunch boxes to the plaza in front of the Daley Civic Center? Park yourselves beneath "Head of a Woman," the massive sculpture constructed by Pablo Picasso, and enjoy free entertainment. Chomp on the sandwich and slurp down the juice as you imbibe performances ranging from drumming to comedy to dance. Events are always changing at this city landmark. Call for a schedule of performances.

Age Range: All ages.
Hours: Summer weekdays at 12 noon. **Admission:** Free.
Time Allowance: One hour.
Directions: Loop area.
Parking: Pay-lots and short-term meters. **Wheelchair Accessible:** Yes.
Restaurant: No, but nearby
Picnicking: Yes. **Rest Rooms:** No. **Gift Shop:** No.

CHICAGO WATER TOWER
Water Tower Park
806 North Michigan Avenue
Chicago, IL 60611
(312) 744-2400

FUN SCALE

Okay, so it's not the *most* fun stop on the planet for kids, but the Chicago Water Tower functions as a Visitor Center, where you can get a wealth of information, and it's one of Chicago's most cherished landmarks. Designed in 1871 by William W. Boyington, it was built to equalize the water pressure for the *Pumping Station* across the street. These two buildings then worked together to supply Chicago with water.

Burlington designed the tower to conceal a standpipe used to even out the water surges, caused by pumping, and keep the water flowing. He concealed the standpipe inside the shell of a medieval castle. Look up at the slender, saw-toothed towers with minarets: Are you in Mecca or the center of Chicago?

Today, the gothic-revival stone tower is also a memorial to the Great Chicago Fire of 1871, being one of the few structures that remained unscathed. Currently, it houses the *Welcome Center* of the *Chicago Office of Tourism*. Inside, you'll find maps, brochures, and friendly staff who are willing to answer questions.

Age Range: Any age. **Hours:** Monday through Friday 9:30 A.M. to 6:00 P.M. Saturday 10:00 A.M. to 6:00 P.M. Sunday 11:00 A.M. to 5:00 P.M. **Admission:** Free. **Time Allowance:** 20 minutes. **Directions:** Near North **Parking:** Meters and pay-lots. **Wheelchair Accessible:** No. **Restaurant:** No, but nearby. **Picnicking:** Yes. **Rest Rooms:** No. **Gift Shop:** No.

FAO SCHWARTZ
840 North Michigan Avenue
Chicago, IL 60611
(312) 587-5000

FUN SCALE

Step into FAO Schwarz and you've entered a world of toys. Rumor has it that it's more difficult getting the parents to leave than the kids. From Barbie to Stretch Cunningham, from Balzac to giant blocks, you'll find many of our culture's commercial icons.

Power Rangers may be cool, but teddy bears are still a favorite. Squeeze a stuffed teddy yourself! Try on a ballet suit or a long flowing gown in the **Dress Up Area**. Step across the giant piano-key walkway and create music as you walk. Enter the **Time Zone** and watch time pass.

Although purchasing toys is tempting, it's not a prerequisite for a visit to the vast world of toys.

Age Range: Any age. **Hours:** Monday through Friday 10:00 A.M. to 7:00 P.M., Saturday and Sunday 11:00 A.M. to 6:00 P.M. **Admission:** Free. **Time Allowance:** Variable, depending on age and shopping interests. **Directions:** Near North. **Parking:** Pay-lots. **Wheelchair Accessible:** Yes. **Restaurant:** No. **Picnicking:** No. **Rest Rooms:** Yes.

HERE'S CHICAGO!
163 EAST PEARSON
CHICAGO, IL 60611
(312) 467-7114

FUN SCALE

Take a captivating one-hour tour of Chicago. Begin with a brief walking tour of the historic **Water Tower Pumping Station**. The pumping station is one of the two buildings that survived the Great Chicago Fire of 1871, and it's still active today. Continue into **The Hall of Flames**, and experience the audio animatronics of an old Irish fisherman describing the fire. See Mrs. O'Leary milking her cow, Daisy, in the barn where the fire first started back in 1871. Stroll past the diorama of the St. Valentine's Massacre and re-live the story of "Bugs" Moran's mob being wiped out by Al Capone. Learn some facts about the Chicago Gangster Era.

Step into the two-hundred-seat theater featuring *Heartbeat Chicago* and experience a fifteen-minute computerized, slide-projector show of Chicagoans talking about their city's architecture, museums, sports, restaurants, and distinct neighborhoods.

Proceed into **Theater II** where audio-animatronic Abe Lincoln will take you through the *City of Dreams* via an awesome helicopter flight over the city. It's all done on a gigantic screen with Dolby sound. Soar over rivers and lakes, bump over train tracks, zip around high-rise buildings. This is a good introduction to Chicago.

Age Range: 8 and older. **Hours:** Open daily. Shows run hourly 10:00 A.M. to 4:30 P.M., Monday through Thursday. Shows run every 1/2 hour 10:00 A.M. to 5:00 P.M., Friday through Sunday. Closed Thanksgiving, Christmas, and New Years Day. **Admission:** Adults $5.75; seniors, students, and children (12 and under) $4.40; families $15.00. **Time Allowance:** 1 hour. **Directions:** Near North. **Parking:** Pay-lots. **Wheelchair Accessible:** Yes. **Restaurant:** Snackbar only. **Picnicking:** No, but nearby. **Rest Rooms:** Yes. **Gift Shop:** Yes; T-shirts, caps, maps.

MUSEUM OF CONTEMPORARY ART
237 East Ontario Street
Chicago, IL 60611-3236
(312) 280-5161

FUN SCALE

Museum Of Contemporary Art

© Copyright Museum of Contemporary Art

What? Ping-Pong racquets covered with empty cans and wads of dough? Black paint splatterings on a white canvas? Stuffed animals on a table? Is that art?

This museum offers a solid introduction to the often hard-to-understand world of contemporary art. Keeping up with the active art world, exhibits are constantly changing. The work displayed is often provocative, daring, and eye-opening. From Jackson Pollock to Francis Bacon, from Pablo Picasso to Andy Warhol, thought-provoking images spark interest and induce questioning among both young and old.

Innovative exhibits promote sculpture, painting, crafts, graphics, video, photography, and performance art. You might call first to see whether it's an appropriate exhibit for kids before venturing out. Guided tours are given throughout the year. (See times listed below.) They last for about forty-five-minutes and change with the exhibits. Although they aren't necessarily geared toward kids, the guides are flexible enough to answer any kid-thrown questions. There is a lag time between exhibits, when there is no tour.

Family Days, involving both children and adults, happen during July and August. On these occasions, hands-on or interactive events take place, ranging from *Modeling the Museum*, which involves the use of sticks or rubber bands, to learning about form and function, to the *Museum Menagerie*, where kids create a performance based on animals found in various works of art.

Special kid tours also occur during the Family Days.

Presently, the Museum of Contemporary Art is in a relatively small facility; however, it is scheduled to relocate to 234 Chicago Avenue in the summer of 1996. The larger, five-level museum will rest on two acres in a park-like setting on Michigan Avenue's Magnificent Mile.

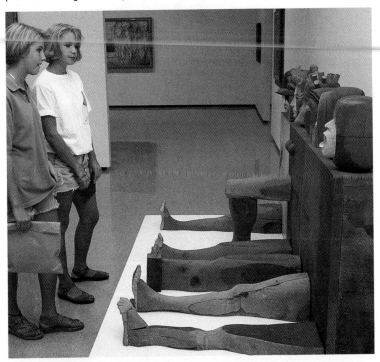

Age Range: Some tours are more fun than others for 7 and under. Call ahead and ask about current ones. Eight and up are more likely to appreciate the art by itself. **Hours:** Tuesday through Saturday from 10:00 A.M. to 5:00 P.M.; Sunday from 12 noon to 5:00 P.M.; closed Monday. *Tour times:* Tuesday through Friday 12:15 P.M.; Saturday and Sunday 1:00 and 3:00 P.M. **Admission:** Adults $5.00, seniors and students $2.50, children (12 and under) free. Tuesdays free. **Time Allowance:** About an hour. **Directions:** Near North. **Parking:** Meters and pay-lots. **Wheelchair Accessible:** Yes. **Restaurant:** Coffee bar only. **Picnicking:** No. **Rest Rooms:** Yes. **Gift Shop:** Yes; cool jewelry, toys, glass bottle stops.

NIKETOWN
669 North Michigan Avenue
Chicago, IL 60611
(312) 642-6363

FUN SCALE

It's more than a sneaker store. It's an "attitude," and an attitude that shouldn't be missed.

"Just do it,"–step into the "attitude" and you're greeted by models of athletes and bicycles, the latter dangling from the ceiling. Colorful fish swim in a tank lining the wall behind a sneaker case (Those sneakers do have a way of sneaking in, don't they?) Memorabilia of popular athletes decorate the gigantic store. After further exploration of the first floor, where you'll discover cycling, running, volleyball, and water sports paraphernalia, climb to the second floor and look through golf, tennis, and basketball attire. On the third floor find kid's stuff, posters, and a *Video Theater* where sports action is shown non-stop on a giant screen.

Age Range: Any age. **Hours:** 10:00 A.M. to 8:00 P.M., Monday through Friday; 9:30 A.M. to 6:00 P.M., Saturday; 10:00 A.M. to 6:00 P.M., Sunday. **Admission:** Free. **Time Allowance:** Variable. **Directions:** Near North. **Parking:** Pay-lot. **Wheelchair Accessible:** Yes. **Restaurant:** No. **Picnicking:** No. **Rest Rooms:** Yes.

JOHN HANCOCK CENTER OBSERVATORY
875 North Michigan Avenue
Chicago, IL 60611
(312) 751-3681

FUN SCALE 🎈🎈🎈🎈

Weeeee! Stop into the world's fastest elevator and shoot up to the **observation deck** on the ninety-fourth floor. The whole journey takes a whopping thirty-nine seconds. Yawn a few times, step off the elevator, and enjoy a breathtaking view of the city.

Drop a quarter into the telescope and see a closer version of what's below. See views of up to eighty miles in all directions. To the north, see Lake Shore Drive Lincoln Park. Spot any giraffes? Look east and see Lake Michigan. It's usually active with sailboats and cruisers. To the south, pick out Chicago's famous Loop. See the Sears Tower? You can't miss it. Try to pick out the many cultural neighborhoods to the west.

The John Hancock ranks as Chicago's second-tallest building, behind the Sears Tower. The exterior skin is composed of aluminum and glass–11,459 panes of glass, to be exact. Feel safe when you think of the 46,000 tons of steel supporting you, as you gaze out over four states–Illinois, Indiana, Wisconsin, and Michigan from a quarter-mile above the ground! By the way, the view is better from John Hancock than Sears Tower, because you can get closer to the windows and look straight down. (Yikes!)

Age Range: Any age. **Hours:** 9:00 A.M. to midnight daily. **Admission:** Adults $4.75, seniors $4.00, children (5-17) $3.25, military free. **Time Allowance:** 30 to 60 minutes. **Directions:** Near North. **Parking:** Pay-lots. **Wheelchair Accessible:** Yes. **Restaurant:** Yes, and snackbar. **Picnicking:** No. **Rest Rooms:** Yes, with changing tables. **Gift Shop:** Yes; posters, T-shirts, postcards.

TERRA MUSEUM OF AMERICAN ART
664 North Michigan Avenue
Chicago, IL 60611
(312) 664-3939

FUN SCALE

"The art of a nation kindles the spirit of its people."
—Daniel J. Terra, founder of the Terra Museum of American Art

Devoted solely to the work of American artists, this museum contains eighteenth, nineteenth, and twentieth-century art. A permanent collection of over four hundred works by artists including Andrew Wyeth, Frank Stella, Mary Cassatt, John Singer Sargent, and Milton Avery share the walls with touring exhibitions. Seven spacious galleries, connected by an internal network of ramps, change exhibits every two or three months.

Call first to see if there's a tour for kids already set up. If not, it's possible to arrange one of your own (Docent reservations must be made with a minimum of ten people.) Ask at the main desk for a *parent/teacher's pamphlet*, which will make your self-guided tour much more enlightening and enjoyable.

Every two or three months, at the start of each new exhibit, **Family Fair** for both children and adults takes place on Sunday afternoons. The two-hour program combines an interactive tour with a gallery activity and hands-on art project. It's a great chance for the whole family to explore and create together.

Age Range: 8 and up for the museum, 5 and up for the Family Fairs. **Hours:** Tuesday 12 noon to 8:00 P.M.; Wednesday through Saturday 10:00 A.M. to 5:00 P.M.; Sunday 12 noon to 5:00 P.M. Closed Monday. **Admission:** Suggested museum donation: Adults $3.00, seniors $2.00, children (12-18) $1.00. Tuesdays and first Sunday of every month admission is free. *Family Fair:* $1.00 per person. **Time Allowance:** About 1 hour. **Directions:** Near North. **Parking:** Meters and pay-lots. **Wheelchair Accessible:** Yes. **Restaurant:** No. **Picnicking:** No. **Rest Rooms:** Yes. **Gift Shop:** Yes; mugs, posters, stationary.

© Copyright Terra Museum of American Art

THE PEACE MUSEUM
350 West Ontario Street
Fourth Floor, Chicago, IL 60610
(312) 440-1860

FUN SCALE

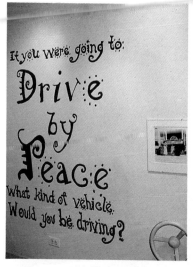

"If we are to reach the real peace in this world and if we are to carry on a real war against war, we shall have to begin with the children."
–Mahatma Gandhi

Visit the only museum in this country dedicated to promoting peace through exposure to the arts and humanities. Thought-provoking and message-sending exhibits spark ideas for solutions through hands-on experience. Although the museum operates with limited resources, its mission is clear–to create non-violent conflict resolution and bring about peace in the world.

Mahatma Gandhi was right, of course: Children *are* the right age for humanistic indoctrination. The museum gives them a chance to do activities such as dress in a foreign costume and take a Polaroid self-portrait–that is, to see what it feels like to be someone else. Or they can write a letter to another country's peace museum, play with puppets and act out questions like, "How would Barney or the Incredible Hulk act in certain situations?" These are activities which make you think.

Other exhibits include artifacts from musicians who have worked for social change. The library contains documentary films, videos, books, and photographs. Check out John Lennon's guitar and U2's hand-written lyrics.

Call ahead for information about the current exhibit.

Age Range: A little something for most ages, varying with the exhibit. Call ahead. **Hours:** 11:00 A.M. to 5:00 P.M., Tuesday through Saturday. Closed major holidays. **Admission:** Adults $3.50, seniors and children $2.00 (suggested donation). **Time Allowance:** 30 to 60 minutes. **Directions:** River North. **Parking:** Meters and pay-lots. **Wheelchair Accessible:** Yes. **Restaurant:** No, but nearby. **Picnicking:** No. **Rest Rooms:** Yes. **Gift Shop:** Yes; T-shirts, mugs, books.

CAPONE'S CHICAGO
605 North Clark Street
Chicago, IL 60610
(312) 654-1919

FUN SCALE

Here, there's no need to stifle yawns.

Experience the sights, sounds, and smells in a 3-D reenactment of scenes from Prohibition in a city where Al Capone's legacy lives on. The half-hour multimedia show tells the "true story" of the gangster era. You're hosted by twelve Disneyish robotic models of historical figures including Al Capone, Bugsy Moran, and Herbert Hoover.

Experience the period in a circular multi-media room featuring "three-dimensional" sound. You'll hear Louis Armstrong play his trumpet and see the intense concentration in his captivating face. The creak of Al Capone's chair and the smell of his cigar smoke help bring alive his story of the crimes in his sordid past. Bullets whizz past your ears, a glowing cross, made of stone, crashes to the ground, and the city shakes beneath your feet.

The show takes you from 1871 to 1933, exposing the birth of Prohibition, the antics and lifestyles of Chicago's gangsters, and the demise of Al Capone. It ends on an upbeat note with stunning scenes of present-day Chicago.

Don't forget to look at the 1926 Buick with a dark history, Carry Nation's (the temperance leader's) bible, and Al Capone's fedora hat. Each is located in the lobby.

Age Range: Nothing is interactive, but the changing robotics hold the interest of 8 and up. **Hours:** 10:00 A.M. to 10:00 P.M. daily. Shows every half hour. **Admission:** Adults $4.75, seniors and children (under 12) $3.75. **Time Allowance:** 45 minutes. **Directions:** Near North. **Parking:** Pay-lots. **Wheelchair Accessible:** Yes. **Restaurant:** Snack bar only. **Picnicking:** No. **Rest Rooms:** Yes. **Gift Shop:** Yes; fedora hats, blow-up machine guns, sweatshirts.

CHICAGO HARD ROCK CAFE

63 West Ontario
Chicago, IL 60610
(312) 943-2252

FUN SCALE

Hip, hot, and happening, the Chicago Hard Rock Cafe explodes with the sound of rock 'n' roll. A popular spot, the lines at times are long; but the music is throbbing and people of all ages are having a good time. You can't miss it. Landmarked by a gigantic guitar towering above, and surrounded by Rock 'n' Roll McDonalds and Capone's Chicago, it's easily found.

On entering the building, you'll find guitars and other rock 'n' roll memorabilia decorating the walls. Dubbed by Andy Warhol as "the Smithsonian of rock 'n' roll," it's home to the instruments of such greats as Lennie Kravitz, Danny Partridge, and the Psychedelic Furs. Look around at the photos documenting rock 'n' roll's past and present.

Actually, the cafe chain began as a burger joint that was designed to provide rock 'n' roll entertainment while customers ate. Chomp on a cheeseburger, slurp down a milkshake, and watch the huge video screen while music permeates the air.

Age Range: Any age. **Hours:** Weekdays 11:00 A.M. to 11:00 P.M.; Saturday 11:00 A.M. to 12:00 midnight; Sunday 11:30 A.M. to 10:00 P.M. **Admission:** Free to sit. Pay to eat. **Time Allowance:** Varies. **Directions:** River North. **Parking:** Meters and pay-lots. **Wheelchair Accessible:** Yes. **Restaurant:** Yes. **Picnicking:** No. **Rest Rooms:** Yes, with changing tables. **Gift Shop:** Yes; cool jackets, pins, T-shirts.

ROCK 'N' ROLL MCDONALDS
600 North Clark Street,
Chicago, IL 60610
(312) 664-7940

FUN SCALE 🎈🎈🎈

In search of fast food or not, you'll find Rock 'n' Roll McDonalds is worth a stop. Even if you don't purchase food, a stroll through the eatery is allowed, day or night. And there's plenty to absorb. The place is jam-packed with rock 'n' roll and period memorabilia–license plates, juke boxes, record albums, life-size Beatle models, and neon galore.

Chomp on a burger as you listen to the beat of Elvis wailing about his blue suede shoes, or the Beach Boys singing about surfer girls. Pop into the old-time photo booth for a shot of you and your friends. Check out the '59 Corvette named *Peggy Sue* after the Buddy Holly hit song.

This McDonalds is generally packed and has a happy atmosphere, but there never seems to be a waiting line, as there is at the neighboring Hard Rock Cafe and Planet Hollywood.

Age Range: All ages. **Hours:** 24 hours a day, 365 days a year. **Admission:** Free. **Time Allowance:** Varies. **Directions:** River North. **Parking:** Free-lot. **Wheelchair Accessible:** Yes. **Restaurant:** Yes. **Picnicking:** No. **Rest Rooms:** Yes. **Gift Shop:** No.

PLANET HOLLYWOOD
633 North Wells Street
Chicago, IL 60610
(312) 266-STAR

FUN SCALE

You can't miss it. Surrounded by palm trees, light beams, speckled stars, and a giant planet towering over the neighboring buildings, Planet Hollywood stands out.

Notice the **handprint wall** as you enter. Can you locate palm prints of Mel Gibson, Goldie Hawn, Demi Moore, and Jimmy Stewart?

Inside you'll find the **movie memorabilia** in a collection of hundreds of artifacts. See an official Teenage Mutant Ninja Turtle suit, Kevin Costner's bat from *Field of Dreams*, Darth Vader's helmet from *Star Wars*, and Demi Moore's potter's wheel from the memorable *Ghosts* scene–to name just a few.

Slurp down a "Home Alone," the kid version of a strawberry daiquiri, or chomp on a piece of Arnold Schwartzenegger's mother's renowned Apple Strudel. Enjoy the tunes of movie soundtracks and watch custom-designed videos showing on a giant screen. A full menu is available, highlighting Californiaish dishes–vegetarian burgers, exotic salads, and weird pastas.

Planet Hollywood is owned by Bruce Willis, Arnold Schwartzenegger, and Sylvester Stallone–so be forewarned that at any time a celebrity may stroll past your table!

Age Range: Any age needs to eat, but 8 and up will appreciate the Hollywood glitz. **Hours:** *Summer*–10:00 A.M. to 1:00 A.M. daily. *Winter*–11:00 A.M. to 12:00 A.M. daily. **Admission:** Free to sit. Pay to eat. **Time Allowance:** Varied. **Directions:** Near North. **Parking:** Meters and pay-lots. **Wheelchair Accessible:** Yes. **Restaurant:** Yes. **Picnicking:** No. **Rest Rooms:** Yes. **Gift Shop:** Yes; sweatshirts, caps, jackets. *Cool Tip:* Although it's not quite as *cool* to go during the day, the lines are shorter or non-existent on weekdays before 5:00 P.M. Reservations are not accepted.

NAVY PIER
600 East Grand Avenue
Chicago, IL 60611
(312) 791-PIER

FUN SCALE

Opened in 1916, the Navy Pier has a long history. It was built to relieve water traffic congestion along the Chicago River. In addition, it was designed to serve as a public recreation facility. Over the years the pier underwent several changes as it became the site of a Navy Mechanics Training School, and then a world-class port facility. (And it was 700 miles away from the ocean!) Since then the Pier, through a $150 million renovation project, has evolved into a place of entertainment for all ages.

Putting history aside, the pier extends five-eighths of a mile out over Lake Michigan and offers a wide range of possibility for fun. Bicycles can be rented, fishing rods can be cast, food munched, and live entertainment experienced. Venture out to the end and look back at the city skyline. (Dramatic!)

The Family Pavilion, on the sound side of the pier, is the new location of the **Chicago Children's Museum** and **IMAX® Theater**, as well as shops and restaurants. Just beyond are the **Crystal Gardens**, an indoor tropical botanical park with fountains and plants galore. In winter, the enclosed **ice skating rink** is open to skaters, while in summer a **carousel**, a 150-foot-high **Ferris wheel**, and a **children's play area** fill the space. The **Skyline Stage** hosts a variety of live entertainment for all ages, from rock 'n' roll to smooth jazz to African dance.

Age Range: Any age. **Hours:** Generally 6:00 A.M. to 8:00 P.M. daily. **Admission:** Free. **Time Allowance:** Varies. **Directions:** Near North. **Parking:** Pay-garage. **Wheelchair Accessible:** Yes. **Restaurant:** Yes, several. **Picnicking:** Yes. **Rest Rooms:** Yes. **Gift Shop:** Yes, many.

SKYLINE STAGE - NAVY PIER
Chicago, Illinois

© Copyright Navy Pier

CHICAGO CHILDREN'S MUSEUM
North Pier
465 East Illinois Street
Chicago, IL 60611
(312) 527-1000

FUN SCALE

You can indeed, as the sign says, "Play with Your Brain" at the Chicago Children's Museum. Kids are encouraged here to look, touch, smell, think, explore, question, and s-t-r-e-t-c-h their brains.

Starting on the first floor, concern yourself with our planet's scarce resources. Crawl *through* a landfill. See a worm farm. Become a garbologist and learn about trash in **The Stinking Truth About Garbage** exhibit. Make a masterpiece out of rubbish and, afterwards, take it home. Experience the magic of effervescence in **The Art and Science of Bubbles**. Create something with the zillions of Legos and check out the models by famous architects. If you're under six, **Touchy Business** is the place for you. It's a

sensory stimulating environment consisting of a *Tactile Tunnel*, a *Fantasy Vehicle*–an airplane/boat/tractor all-in-one–and *Three Bears' Cabin*.

On the second floor you'll find **NEWSbrief!**, a

TV studio for kids eight and older designed to teach critical thinking while learning about news production. Broadcast your own show and see yourself on the big screen. Reporter wanna-bes, now's your chance!

City Hospital is designed to dispel children's fears of doctors and hospitals through hands-on experience with displays dealing with human anatomy, health, and nutrition. In the **Wheelchair Skill Course** kids can play wheelchair basketball to heighten awareness of physical disabilities and challenges.

The **Grandparents** exhibit celebrates your parent's parents in a big way. Use the computer to create a family tree and learn to say "grandma" or "grandpa" in other languages. Also, step into the colorful world of **Magic and Masquerades**. Listen to the music of West Africa and then create your own. Bang on the drums! Draw yourself. Weave something. Design your own West African jewelry.

The museum reaches out to a diverse community of children from all socio-economic and ethnic background. Many of the signs are bilingual, written in English and Spanish.

As of the summer of 1995, the Chicago Children's Museum will be relocated on the Navy Pier in a much bigger space.

Age Range: 2 to 12. **Hours:** Tuesday through Friday from 12:30 to 4:30 P.M. (pre-school exhibit opens at 10:00 A.M.); Saturday and Sunday from 10:30 A.M. to 4:30 P.M.; Thursday, from 5:00 to 8:00 P.M., is Free Family Night.
Admissions: Adults $3.50, seniors and children (1 to 12) $2.50. **Time Allowance:** 1 1/2 to 2 hours.
Directions: Near North. **Parking:** Meter and pay-lots. Pay-lot discounts available at adjacent lots with tickets validated at the museum. **Wheelchair Accessible:** Yes. **Restaurant:** Yes. **Picnicking:** No. **Rest Rooms:** Yes, with changing tables. **Gift Shop:** Yes; volcano kits, stuffed animals, caps.

BICYCLE MUSEUM OF AMERICA
North Pier
435 East Illinois Street
Chicago, IL 60611
(312) 222-0500

FUN SCALE

Situated in North Pier Festival Market lies something of an oddity–a bicycle museum. But what better place for it than a city that was considered the hub of the bicycle industry at the turn of the century?

Begin your visit by watching a short video based on the history of bicycles. Follow it with a self-guided tour past hundreds of bicycles from a 50,000-item collection. The bikes are arranged chronologically, from the mid-1800s to the present. Check out the fat balloon-tires of the 1940s and 1950s. Gawk at the flowered-banana seats and sissy bars of the 1960s. Admire the sleek racing machines of today.

Nothing is hands-on or interactive here, but the exhibits will maintain the interest of bicycle fans. Exhibits change from time to time.

Age Range: Nothing is interactive. 7 and up. **Hours:** Monday through Saturday 10:00 A.M. to 9:00 P.M.; Sunday 11:00 A.M. to 6:00 P.M. **Admission:** Adults $4.00; seniors, students, children (5-13) $2.00. **Time Allowance:** 30 minutes. **Directions:** North Pier. **Parking:** Pay-lots and meters. **Wheelchair Accessible:** Yes. **Restaurant:** Yes. **Picnicking:** No. **Rest Rooms:** Yes. **Gift Shop:** No.

LINCOLN PARK CONSERVATORY
2400 North Stockton Drive
Chicago, IL 60614
(312) 294-4770

FUN SCALE

Take a short safari through a jungle of exotic plants abutting the zoo in Lincoln Park. Classical music serenades you in the greenhouses of lush flora.

Enter the **Palm House** where a display of rare orchids from many countries greets you. Continue on, and you're surrounded by banana trees, tapioca plants, and rubber trees. The fishtail palm, native to India, yields about three gallons of wine a day for several weeks, making it a valuable crop.

Cross into the **Fern House** where birdnest ferns, vanilla vines, and cycads live. Cycads, from the Mesozoic period, are among the oldest plants (about 135 million years, give or take a few). They are the "link" between flowerless and flowering plants.

The **Show House** offers four major exhibits annually. The *Christmas Show* runs through the Christmas holidays, the *Azalea Show* occurs in early March, the *Easter Show* in spring, and the *Chrysanthemum Show* in November. Each lasts for about three weeks.

In the **Cactus House**, you'll find cacti and succulent plants living in a southwestern desert landscape of sponge rocks and sand. The Old Man cactus has long silvery hair. Can you guess why *Opuntia microdasys* is commonly called "prickly pear?" *Aloe vera* is an important plant used for medicinal purposes. Try rubbing it on your skin after getting burned. It really takes the pain away!

Age Range: Any age. **Hours:** 10:00 A.M. to 5:00 P.M. daily. Open 9:00 A.M. to 5:00 P.M., December 24 through 31. **Admission:** Free. **Time Allowance:** 20 to 30 minutes. **Directions:** Lincoln Park. **Parking:** Meters. **Wheelchair Accessible:** Yes. **Restaurant:** No, but nearby. **Picnicking:** Yes. **Rest Rooms:** Yes. **Gift Shop:** No.

LINCOLN PARK ZOO
2200 North Cannon Drive
Chicago, IL 60614
(312) 294-4660

FUN SCALE

A visit to Lincoln Park Zoo means an adventure in other worlds–the wilds of Africa, the bush of Australia, and the mid-western American farm site. The fact that admission is always free is only one reason why it's the "most visited zoo in the nation."

Several outstanding programs exist for children. The **Pritzker Children's Zoo** is actually a zoo within a zoo. Learn how people, plants, and animals share the world here. Check out the baby owls and newly hatched chicks in the *Pritzker Nursery*. The *Discovery Carts* circulate from

time to time with adaptation and conservation-oriented exhibits. Have you ever touched an iguana? Now's the time. In *Conservation Station*, study a bat x-ray, or compare an x-ray of a man's hand with that of a gorilla's. (It's amazingly close!)

Situated right smack in the middle of Chicago, **Farm-in-the-Zoo** seems somewhat out of place. The five-acre farm, a model of a Midwestern farmstead, is a wonderful spot to get a taste of country life. The *Dairy Barn* is home to the cows and a place to see milking demonstrations. Piglets live in the *Livestock Barn*. (Everyone loves the piggies!) See chicks hatch in the *Poultry Barn*. In the *Horse Barn* you'll find gigantic Clydesdale horses and silky Shetland ponies, and in the *Main Barn* you can churn butter and sample a taste of goat's milk. (Mmmm!)

The **Lester E. Fisher Great Ape House**, a reconstruction of a rain forest setting, houses one of the world's finest collections of primates. Gorillas, orangutans, and chimps all share the same naturalistic environment.

Watch penguins waddle to the cliff's edge and take the plunge into the water below as birds swoop overhead at the **Penguin and Seabird House**.

The **Large Mammal Area** is where the big guys live. Elephants, hippos, rhinos, and giraffes roam about the outdoor habitats. Discover the underwater viewing windows, and watch the polar bear drop in for an occasional dip.

Koalas are cute but shy creatures. If you're lucky, you'll spot them climbing in the trees of **Koala Plaza**. Seeing them is definitely worth a try!

Gibbons, mandrills, and marmosets live in the indoor rain forest of the **Helen Brach Primate House**. In the *Hands-on Center* you can touch skulls and fur.

Home to the endangered and threatened big cats is the **Kovler Lion House**. Watch startlingly-beautiful creatures including leopards, tigers, lions, and cheetahs as they prowl around the rocks in agitated circles.

Zooadventures take place throughout the year and range in programs from animal-mask making and getting to know a boa constrictor snake, to something as wild as learning about canine-enforcement at the U.S. Customs Service. Workshops, which cost an added fee, are appropriate for age three and up. Call for specifics.

Age Range: Any age. **Hours:** *General Zoo*–9:00 A.M. to 5:00 P.M. daily. *Pritzker Children's Zoo Programs*–10:00 A.M. to 2:00 P.M. weekdays, 10:00 A.M. to 4:00 P.M. weekends. **Admission:** Free. **Time Allowance:** 1 to 3 hours. **Directions:** Lincoln Park. **Parking:** Pay-lot during summer and weekends off-season only; otherwise, parking is free. **Wheelchair Accessible:** Yes. Wheelchairs and stroller rentals available. **Restaurant:** Yes. **Picnicking:** Yes. **Rest Rooms:** Yes, some with changing tables. **Gift Shop:** Yes; T-shirts, film, stuffed animals.

CHICAGO ACADEMY OF SCIENCES
2001 North Clark Street
Chicago, IL 60614
(312) 549-0606

FUN SCALE

Walk inside and enter the great outdoors where you'll experience millions of years of life. Stroll through the cool, dark *coal forest*, a replication of one 300 million years ago when Chicago was a tropical jungle.

Climb the staircase to the second floor and step into a world of pillars covered with tree bark and walls lined with trees. Animal tracks wind across the floor, while stars dot the ceiling. A gigantic stuffed buffalo stands majestically as if on guard. Around the periphery are life-like *dioramas* filled with plants

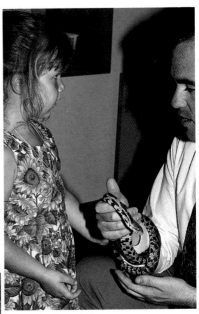

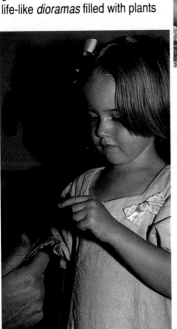

and animals native to the Midwest during the early 1900s. Listen to the waterfall spilling on the ground. Step into the walk-through *Illinois cave*. It's filled with stalactites and stalagmites. (By the way, stalactites hang down and stalagmites grow upward.)

On the third floor you're immediately greeted at the head of the steps by a humongous white polar bear standing on its hind legs. Say hello and continue to the seventy five year-old **Atwood Celestial Sphere**. Step inside and gaze at the stars of the Chicago sky. Push the button and change the view from night stars to day stars. Kids

love the **Children's Gallery**. It's an area full of "touchables"– including even snakes and turtles, at certain times. Crawl inside the giant sea turtle shell and imagine what it would be like to live in such a home. Learn how animals are instinctively architects. Play a natural history game, identify fossils from the fossil drawer, or create a puppet show. Organized **Puppet Shows** take place two times a day, Saturday through Monday, and provide entertainment usually dealing with science-related themes.

The big exhibits based on timely environmental issues change annually. In *DinoRama!*, life-like robotic dinosaurs growl and prowl. *Water Works* gives you a sampling of the ecology of the Chicago River. It's a large sandbox of sorts, in which running water creates flooding and meandering streams. Learn about pH levels and the effect of zebra mussels on the ecosystem. *Nature's Fury* offers a wild and interactive experience in which tornadoes, floods, and volcanoes are simulated and explored. Put your hands in a swirling and spiraling tornado machine. Step into the earthquake room where you'll experience a shaking that registers 5.5 on the Richter Scale. (Yikes!)

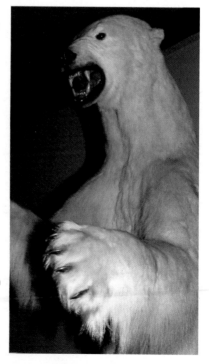

Age Range: 4 and up. **Hours:** 10:00 A.M. to 5:00 P.M. daily. Closed Christmas Day. **Admission:** Adults $2.00, seniors and children (3 to 17) $1.00. Mondays free. **Time Allowance:** 1 or 2 hours. **Directions:** Lincoln Park. **Parking:** Meters, pay-lots, and parking garages. **Wheelchair Accessible:** Yes. **Restaurant:** No, but nearby. **Picnicking:** Yes. **Rest Rooms:** Yes. **Gift Shop:** Yes; science toys, books, jewelry.

CHICAGO HISTORICAL SOCIETY
Clark Street at North Avenue
Chicago, IL 60614-4600
(312) 642-4600

FUN SCALE

Relive the past in the first museum built in Chicago. Since 1939, the society has opened its doors and exposed people to Chicago's yesterday. It's a large facility with much to pick and choose from.

Step into the **Illinois Pioneer Life Gallery** and in front of you is Chicago's first locomotive–the *Pioneer*. Climb aboard the twelve-ton train and become the engineer. Watch an eleven-minute laser disc film on the Great Chicago Fire. See "Bessie," a doll who was saved from the fire by a little girl, and melted marbles and spoons.

In the **Chicago History Wing** listen to three-minutes of Chicago radio, jazz, blues, and gospel. Check out the *Showcase of Chicago's Firsts*. It's full of Tootsie Rolls, Lincoln Logs, and lava lamps. Did you know that the very first McDonald's Restaurant was built in Illinois? The eight *Chicago Dioramas* are a favorite of both the young and old. See miniature scenes of Chicago life from 1795 to 1893. The lighting is fantastic, especially in the Great Chicago Fire scene. See Walter Payton's football jersey in the small *History of Sports* exhibit.

Pick up a *Gallery Guide* and go into the **American History Wing**. In *"We the People"* see the original copy of the *Declaration of Independence*. There's

68

also an original watercolor sketch of an American flag done in 1779. Just think: That funny looking sketch could have been the flag of today, had people decided differently. Learn about Abraham Lincoln, the Civil War, and slavery through the many exhibits.

In the **Hands-on History Gallery** kids get a feel for history (literally). Step into an early *fur trader's cabin* and pick up a beaver pelt or an old kettle. Did you know that one kettle was worth seven beaver pelts back in the nineteenth century? Touch fire-melted artifacts from the Great Fire. Ride a high-wheeled bicycle. Step into the *Radio Corner* to recreate the old-time sounds of a 1930s radio show. Check out the single-row roller skates from the 1880s, which look surprisingly like the sleek in-line skates of today.

Pick up the *Treasure Hunt for Kids* at the desk in the lobby. It's helpful to keep kids on track and maintain interest throughout the museum, and it works!

Age Range: 5 and up for the Hands-On History Gallery. 9 and up for the other exhibits. **Hours:** Monday through Saturday 9:30 A.M. to 4:30 P.M., Sunday 9:00 A.M. to 5:00 P.M. Closed Thanksgiving, Christmas, and New Years Day. **Admission:** Adults $3.00, seniors (over 65) and students (17 to 22) with ID $2.00, children (6 to 17) $1.00. Mondays are free. **Time Allowance:** 1 to 2 hours. **Directions:** Lincoln Park. **Parking:** Meters and pay-lots. **Wheelchair Accessible:** Yes. A limited number of wheelchairs are available for loan. **Restaurant:** Yes, Big Shoulders Cafe. **Picnicking:** Yes. **Rest Rooms:** Yes. **Gift Shop:** Yes; historic paper dolls, fire engines, books.

PLAYERS WORKSHOP CHILDREN'S THEATRE
2636 North Lincoln Avenue
Chicago, IL 60614 (Summers only) or
Body Politic Theatre
2261 North Lincoln Avenue
Chicago, IL (Off-season)
(312) 929-6288

FUN SCALE

© Copyright Players Workshop Children's Theatre

Twenty-eight years of productions make the Players Workshop Children's Theatre the oldest children's theatre in Chicago. Performances ranging from *Uncle Peter's Russian Folk Tales* to *MenuMania* to *Quoth the Raven* include music and stories that require full-audience participation. Kids are encouraged to shout, scream, and jump up and down (at appropriate times). Shows last about an hour—optimum kid-sitting time.

Watch for the changes in theater location. During the summer, Players Workshop Theatre performs in its own theater; off season, performances take place at a rented space nearby.

© Copyright Players Workshop Children's Theatre

Age Range: 4 and up. **Hours:** Most Sundays at 2:00 P.M. **Admission:** Most shows are $5.00. **Time Allowance:** About an hour. **Directions:** Lincoln Park. **Parking:** Pay-lot. **Wheelchair Accessible:** In summer theater only. **Restaurant:** No, but nearby. **Picnicking:** No, except for special birthday parties. **Rest Rooms:** Yes. **Gift Shop:** No, T-shirts only.

THE PUPPET PARLOR
1922 West Montrose Avenue
Chicago, IL 60613
(312) 774-2919

FUN SCALE

Patterned after European marionette theatres, The Puppet Parlor presents puppet shows in an intimate jewel-box theatre with the puppeteers positioned several feet above the marionettes. Although the facilities border on being well seasoned (to put it gently), performances are entertaining. The lights dim, the orchestra pit rises, the conductor raises his baton, and the show begins.

Children's puppet shows range from *The Beauty and the Beast* to *The Little Mermaid* to *Cinderella* and are colorfully performed. Adult puppet shows such as *Les Petite Follies* and Mozart's *Impresario* happen on weekend nights and are loaded with burlesque, pretty girls, and nostalgia–marionette style. (Ooh la la!)

Age Range: 4 and up. Check first to see which age is appropriate. **Hours:** *Children Performances*–Saturdays and Sundays 2:00 P.M. *Adult Performances*–Saturdays and Sundays 7:00 P.M. For weekday times call (312) 774-2919. **Admission:** $5.00 per person for daytime performances, $10.00 for adult evening shows. **Time Allowance:** About 1 1/2 hours. **Directions:** Ravenswood. **Parking:** Meter. **Wheelchair Accessible:** Yes, for smaller chairs. **Restaurant:** Popcorn and sodas only. **Picnicking:** No. **Rest Rooms:** Yes. **Gift Shop:** Yes; marionettes, hand-puppets, stuffed animals.

WRIGLEY FIELD TOUR
Wrigley Field
1060 West Addison Street
Chicago IL 60613
(312) 404-CUBS

FUN SCALE

What could be more American than a tour of Wrigley Field?

Seven tours per year provide behind-the-scene views of the baseball park. They begin with a brief history of the stadium, followed by a tour through the **Sky Box** which holds sixty-seven mezzanine suites, each with its own TV, fridge, heaters, and a fantastic view. Rental costs range between $65,000 and $90,000 per year with a three-year lease. A mere $2,000 will get you a single sky-box with fifteen seats for a day.

Next, see the **Press Box** and check out the spot where broadcaster Harry Caray *still* sings "Take Me Out to the Ball Game" during the seventh inning stretch. Visit the **Stadium Club**, which holds a semi-fancy restaurant open to season ticket holders only. A stroll through the **Locker Room** offers a view of where showers are taken, cleats are laced, and sweaty uniforms are stashed. You can see the lockers of your favorite players. The **Security Office**, a tour highlight for kids, reveals high-tech equipment that surveys almost every square inch of the field, as well as the neighboring buildings. Cameras have the ability to zoom in when you least expect it. (Look out!) Finally, walk out on the field and see the park from the players' perspective.

Proceeds from the tours go to Cubs Care, youth sports, children with special needs, and education.

Age Range: 6 and up, if a baseball fan. **Hours:** April through September, call for dates and times. **Admission:** $10.00 per person. **Time Allowance:** 1 1/2 hours. **Directions:** Wrigleyville. **Parking:** Free-lot with tour. **Wheelchair Accessible:** Yes. **Restaurant:** No, but nearby. **Picnicking:** No. **Rest Rooms:** Yes. **Gift Shop:** Yes; caps, T-shirts, baseballs.

MEXICAN FINE ARTS CENTER MUSEUM

1852 West 19th Street
Chicago, IL 60603
(312) 738-1503

FUN SCALE

Located in the heart of Pilsen, the largest Mexican community in the Midwest, the Mexican Fine Arts Center Museum bursts with culture. From the most traditional to the avant garde, exhibits provide a window into a rich culture, past and present. Four major gallery shows a year include a range in media, from painting to papier-mâché.

Special programs and celebrations happen throughout the year. A favorite, **El Dia de los Muertos**, or Day of the Dead, reflects a culture that *celebrates* death. The festival is actually an attempt on the part of the people to reconcile life with death. Although foreigners like to compare it to Halloween, there's no comparison. Instead of instilling holy terror, the holiday is both jovial and festive, and death is treated with respect. Traditionally, the festivities start with food preparation and the placement of altars around the house. The procession then moves on to the family cemetery, dropping flower petals along the way. In the cemetery the burial grounds are decorated with flowers, food, and other cherished items. The food is grand and the decorations are wild–a huge party with the dead!

The Day of the Dead exhibits at the museum run from October through early December and change in content from year to year. Demonstrations including *sugar-skull making (calacas)*, *sand painting*, and *tree-of-life decorating* occur from time to time. Call for information.

Two other annual events are **Del Corazon** and **Sor Juana Inez de la Cruz**. Del Corazon, which means "of the heart," takes place around April and lasts for about six weeks. (*Aye carumba*, the Mexicans know how to party!) The significance of Del Corazon for Mexicans living in Chicago is that Chicago is in the "heart" of the Midwest. The heart has traditionally been an important Mexican icon.

Sor Juana Inez de la Cruz happens in November and was named after a Mexican woman who was both a poet and a nun, and who, during the seventeenth century, was one of America's first feminists. (Kudos!) Theater, music, and dance abound, making for colorful and festive events.

Exhibits change quarterly in the museum and recognize a culture *sin fronteras* (without borders), including both traditional and contemporary artistic expressions of Mexico and the Mexican communities of the U.S. *Docent tours* for groups of five or more must be prearranged. Some shows are more fun for kids than others. Call ahead for reservations and information about the current exhibit. *¡Viva Mexico!*

Age Range: Varies with show. Call ahead. **Hours:** 10:00 A.M. to 5:00 P.M. from Tuesday through Sunday. Closed Monday and major holidays. **Admission:** Free. **Time Allowance:** 30 to 60 minutes. **Directions:** Pilsen. **Parking:** Meter. **Wheelchair Accessible:** Yes. **Restaurant:** No. **Picnicking:** Yes. **Rest Rooms:** Yes. **Gift Shop:** Yes; papier-mâché dolls, masks, drums.

COMISKEY PARK TOUR
333 West 35th Street
Chicago, IL 60616
(312) 924-1000 (extension 7182)

FUN SCALE

© Copyright Chicago White Sox

Experience the world of baseball from a different perspective. Go behind-the-scenes in the home of the Chicago White Sox, and see the **Press Box**, where the media work, and the **Locker Rooms**, where Frank Thomas puts black shadow under his eyes and Jack McDowell has his arm worked on before the game. Check out the **Security Office**, where you're always being watched. A knowledgeable guide answers questions and fills you in on the latest baseball trivia.

Walk out on the field and gaze up at the scoreboard which, when a home run is hit, explodes with fireworks. The explosion costs a whopping $2,000 each time.

If you find any cups laying around, pick them up. They are recyclable and are worth coupons toward White Sox merchandise–baseball cards, bricks from the old park, jerseys. What recycling incentive!

Age Range: 5 and up. **Hours:** Tuesday and Friday 10:30 A.M. and 1:30 P.M., year round. (The 1:30 P.M. tour is not available when the team is in town.) Reservations required 10 days in advance. **Admission:** Adults $5.00, seniors and children (14 and under) $3.00. **Time Allowance:** 1 1/2 hours. **Directions:** South of the Loop. **Parking:** Free lot. **Wheelchair Accessible:** Yes. **Restaurant:** No. **Picnicking:** No. **Rest Rooms:** Yes, with changing tables in women's and some men's rooms. **Gift Shop:** Yes; baseball cards, caps, jerseys.

GRAVITY CLIMBING GYM
1935 South Halstead Street
Chicago, IL 60608
(312) 733-5006

FUN SCALE

It's common for kids who are natural-born climbers to feel compelled to scale tall obstacles. At Gravity Climbing Gym they have a chance to tackle a *tall wall* over three stories high. Children under twelve may climb, but must be accompanied by an adult; kids twelve and up may climb alone, but need written parental consent.

Hook up to a rope and harness, find a trustworthy belaying partner, and commence the assent. Follow the course-levels marked by colors (white, yellow, green, or blue) and connected by hand and foot holds. This has a lot to do with teamwork and trust.

Of course, if you're a neophyte, you'll need some instructions to climb the tall wall. Lessons take place on Wednesday nights at 6:30 P.M. and give you a chance to learn from experienced mountain climbers.

Those who prefer to be closer to the ground can *"boulder around"* in the other room. The "boulder" is a wall that's no more than ten feet high and you learn similar skills–minus the ropes.

The space is available for rent, and birthday parties here are always a hit. Call for prices.

Age Range: Any age that can walk can climb, as long as accompanied by an adult. **Hours:** *Summer*–3:00 to 10:00 P.M. during the week, 12 noon to 8:00 P.M. weekends. *Winter*–12 noon to 10:00 P.M. Tuesday through Friday; 12 noon to 8:00 P.M. Friday, Saturday, and Sunday. **Admission:** $10.00 per person for up to four hours of climbing. *Rentals*–of climbing shoes, harness rope, etc. available. Maximum of $8.00 per person for all equipment. *Instructions*–$35.00 per hour. **Time Allowance:** 2 to 3 hours. **Directions:** East Pilsen/Chinatown. **Parking:** Free-lot. **Wheelchair Accessible:** No. **Restaurant:** No. **Picnicking:** No. **Rest Rooms:** Yes. **Gift Shop:** T-shirts and bottled water only. *Cool Tip:* Go right after school. You'll avoid the crowds and get more climbing space.

BALZEKAS MUSEUM OF LITHUANIAN CULTURE
6500 South Pulaski Road
Chicago, IL 60629
(312) 582-6500

FUN SCALE

Sample the culture of another country without leaving Chicago. Although the Balzekas Museum of Lithuanian Culture is not a huge museum, it educates with bits and pieces of a country once dominated by the Soviet Union.

The **Children's Museum of Immigrant History** is divided into two areas—Passport to Lithuania and Castle Quest—separated by a drawbridge. In *Passport to Lithuania*, you can rediscover nineteenth century practices. Knead bread dough. Strum a tune on the ancient *kanklés*. Dress up in ancient folk costumes. Handle nineteenth century kitchen utensils and farm tools. Check out the wooden pitchfork!

Across the bridge, in *Castle Quest*, you can discover Lithuania during the Middle Ages when it was one of the largest and most influential countries in Europe. Step into the Armory and examine authentic chainmail worn by knights. Design your own coat of arms. Transform yourself into a princess or prince with the Castle Wardrobe. Try a hand at the giant armor jigsaw puzzle or build your own castle with Legos.

The main part of the museum, **Lithuania Through the Ages**, spans from 1600 B.C. to the early twentieth century with rotating exhibits. Ceramics, jewelry, painting, armor, folk costumes, and artifacts provide you with a sampling of Lithuania's past.

Age Range: 2 to 8 will appreciate the Children's Museum. 8 and up might appreciate the main museum for limited amounts of time. **Hours:** 10:00 A.M. to 4:00 P.M. daily. **Admission:** Adults $3.00, seniors and students $2.00, children (under 12) $1.00. Free Mondays. **Time Allowance:** About an hour. **Directions:** South of the Loop. **Parking:** Free-lot. **Wheelchair Accessible:** Yes, with one loaner. **Restaurant:** No. **Picnicking:** No. **Rest Rooms:** Yes. **Gift Shop:** Yes; dolls, wood carvings, amber jewelry.

THE DAVID AND ALFRED SMART MUSEUM OF ART
The University of Chicago
5550 South Greenwood Avenue
Chicago, IL 60637
(312) 702-0200

FUN SCALE

Every once in a while a museum comes along and reminds you that it's possible to have exciting exhibitions without their being overwhelming. Located at the University of Chicago, the Smart Museum is a small gem of a museum, and although it has no hands-on activities, it's a good place to catch a glimpse of art–from Chinese Neolithic pots to Greek urns dating 535-520 B.C. to the contemporary paintings of Mark Rothko.

The permanent collection, consisting of 5,000 works, changes four times a year. Tours are available for groups of ten or more and are given by university students. They're geared toward adults more than kids and reservations must be made in advance. I would suggest picking up a "Family Activity Sheet" at the admissions desk. It acts as a guide, and you'll learn some fun facts about the artwork.

Special kid-oriented programs come twice a year. *Family Day* takes place in June and a *Holiday Party* happens in December. Each offers live performances, food, and art projects. There are special kid *Gallery Walks* offered throughout the program days and the festivities are free.

Age Range: There are no hands-on activities or tours geared toward children. Unless with an adult who is willing to explain, or using the "Family Activity Sheet", it's a difficult space for children under 10 years. **Hours:** Tuesday through Friday 10:00 A.M. to 4:00 P.M.; Saturday and Sunday 12 noon to 6:00 P.M. Closed Monday. **Admission:** Free. **Time Allowance:** 45 to 90 minutes. **Directions:** Hyde Park. **Parking:** Free-lot on the corner of 55th Street and Greenwood Avenue on weekends. Pay-lots during weekdays. **Wheelchair Accessible:** Yes. **Restaurant:** No, but nearby. **Picnicking:** Yes. **Rest Rooms:** Yes, with changing tables. **Gift Shop:** Yes; children's art books, jewelry, dominos.

79

DuSABLE MUSEUM OF
AFRICAN AMERICAN HISTORY

740 East 56th Place
Chicago, IL 60637
(312) 947-0600

FUN SCALE

Trace hundreds of years of black history in the DuSable Museum, from its African roots to present-day American shoots. Learn about the struggles and achievements of African-Americans including Malcolm X, Martin Luther King, Rosa Parks, and Marcus Garvey.

Back in 1779, Jean Baptiste DuSable, after whom the museum is named, built a log cabin with his Potawatomi Indian wife along the Chicago River. He established a trading post, traded furs, and is considered Chicago's first citizen.

Exhibits in the museum, although not totally geared toward children, offer a sense of African-American history and culture through murals, sculptures, paintings, videos, and special programs. The time line on the walls illustrates **Generations of Struggle**, which highlights events since 1700. In the **Slave Gallery**, you'll find a room with rusted shackles on the floor and walls. The horrible space depicts life as living death aboard a slave ship.

The injustice of segregation is captured by a Mississippi diner sign that reads, "Whites only. Coloreds use back door."

On a brighter note, the **Harold Washington Wing**, named after

80

Chicago's first black mayor, hosts exhibits by black artists. Changing displays trace black history and illustrate the many accomplishments of African Americans today. In **Treasures of the DuSable,** you can see memorabilia of African-American superstars, such as the boxing gloves of Joe Louis.

Special programs run throughout the year. From Kwanzaa storytelling to performance dance, from children's theater to doll making, the museum is rich in cultural shows. In these special events lie the strength of the museum.

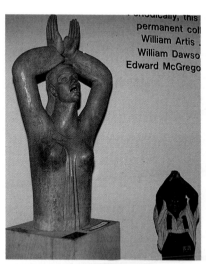

...periodically, this permanent coll
William Artis
William Dawso
Edward McGrego

Age Range: 8 and up unless there are special children's programs. **Hours:** October 1 through April 1, Monday through Saturday, 10:00 A.M. to 4:00 P.M.; Sunday, 12 noon to 4:00 P.M. April 2 through September 30, Monday through Saturday, 10:00 A.M. to 5:00 P.M.; Sunday, 12 noon to 5:00 P.M. **Admission:** Adults $3.00, students and seniors $2.00, children (6-13) $1.00. Free on Thursdays. **Time Allowance:** About 1 hour. **Directions:** Hyde Park. **Parking:** Free-lot. **Wheelchair Accessible:** Yes. **Restaurant:** No. **Picnicking:** Yes. **Rest Rooms:** Yes. **Gift Shop:** Yes; baskets, jewelry, dolls.

MUSEUM OF SCIENCE AND INDUSTRY
57th Street and Lake Shore Drive
Chicago, IL 60637
(312) 684-1414 or (800) 468-6674

FUN SCALE

Anyone who pooh-poohs science and industry, believing them to be complicated, beyond comprehension, and maybe even a little dull, should take a trip to the Museum of Science and Industry. Push buttons, pull levers, pick up telephones, and you will explore this fascinating world.

Changing interactive exhibits aid in simplifying hard-to-understand scientific principles and industrial concepts. With over 2,000 exhibits, there's something for everyone. On the balcony level, learn about the human body. Walk through **The Heart**–a sixteen-foot pulsating model, the beat of which is audible throughout the museum. Experiment with computers and learn how many pumps an average heart beats while playing checkers, running a race, or sleeping. Turn wheels and struggle to make blood go first through a clogged **artery** and then a healthy artery.

Elsewhere, try taking the **Wise Eating Habit Quiz**. Why is it that potato chips are not quite so good for you as lima beans? In **The Brain**, learn about disabilities by watching a video, attention spans by playing "Simon Says," and the perception of space and reasoning through computer games.

A favorite on the second floor is the **subterranean coal mine**. Enter an elevator which lowers you down into the mine where you can ride a train through a shaft. It's dark, damp, and

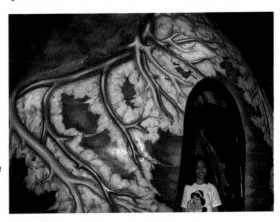

very popular. Auditory phenomena take place in the **Whispering Gallery,** a wonderful exhibit for younger children.

On the ground floor is the **U-505 Submarine,** a German World War II vessel that is completely climbable. **Curiosity Place**, nearby, is the space for children six and under to explore motion, light, sound, and force on a smaller scale.

Scheduled to open in the spring of 1995 is **AIDS: The War Within**. The first permanent exhibit of its kind in the USA, it will promote understanding of the HIV virus; its emphasis is on prevention.

In the **OMNIMAX Theater** you can see startlingly-real films projected on the seventy-six-foot wide, five-story tall screen. Six-channel sound surrounds you in the comfortable seats. You'll watch films of ferocious sharks, sparkling stars, rock 'n' rolling Mick Jagger, and stampeding wildebeest.

Age Range: All ages. **Hours:** *Memorial Day to Labor Day*–9:30 A.M. to 5:30 P.M. daily; 9:30 A.M. to 9:00 P.M. Fridays. *Off-season*–9:30 A.M. to 4:00 P.M. Monday through Friday; 9:30 to 5:30 P.M. Saturday, Sunday, and holidays. Closed Christmas. **Admission:** *General*–Adults $6.00, seniors (over 65) $4.00, children (5-12) $2.50. Free Thursday. *Omnimax (Thursday only)*–Adults $6.00, seniors $5.00, children (5-12) $4.00, infants (4 and under) free on adult lap or $3.00 occupying a seat. *Combo to General and Omnimax Theater*–Adults $10.00, seniors $8.00, children $5.50, infants (4 and under) free on adult lap or $3.00 occupying a seat. **Time Allowance:** 3 hours to full-day. **Directions:** Hyde Park. **Parking:** Free-lot. **Wheelchair Accessible:** Yes. **Restaurant:** Yes. **Picnicking:** Yes. **Rest Rooms:** Yes, with changing tables. **Gift Shop:** Yes; science toys, books, T-shirts. *Cool Tip:* Do the coal mine tour in the morning or late afternoons to avoid lines.

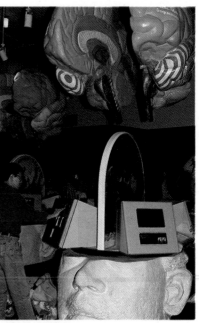

ORIENTAL INSTITUTE MUSEUM
University of Chicago
1155 East 58th Street
Chicago, IL 60637
(312) 702-9520

FUN SCALE 🎈🎈🎈🎈

Stop. Before deciding whether to go to the Oriental Institute Museum, call to see if it's open. As early as July 1995 and as late as spring 1996, the institute is scheduled to close for about a year for major renovations. The $10 million project will provide climate control and more space.

If the museum *is* open, it's well worth a visit. Located in the heart of the University of Chicago, it houses a treasure of towering statues, mummies, and artifacts from the Near East.

Many of the items, which date from 9000 B.C. to the tenth century A.D., were unearthed by archaeologists from the University of Chicago at the turn of

this century. Through the museum's five galleries, discover the invention of writing, the birth of ancient cities, and the beginnings of the arts and sciences, and religion.

In the **Egyptian Gallery**, you'll see examples of hieroglyphic writing, as well as tombs and temples.

Check out the mysterious symbols that cover the mummy case of Lady Meresamon at the end of the hall.

The Assyrian exhibit actually begins at the end of the Egyptian Gallery. You can't miss the giant human-headed, winged bull that was found in an Assyrian palace. The **Assyrian Gallery** holds a collection of carved-stone reliefs. Horses, valued highly, were carved with elaborate trappings and feathers on their heads.

In the **Mesopotamian Gallery**, you'll find evidence of a culture that developed the wheel, plow, and sail. You'll also see carvings of speared lions, because the Mesopotamian kings hunted them as a royal sport. A bull's head that weighs ten tons is in the **Persian Gallery.**

Although the Oriental Institute is not an interactive museum, there are several ways to make the visit more kid-intensive. Ten cents buys a *Gallery Adventure Sheet*, and they're worth the dime; two versions, each for a different age group, are available. *Treasure Hunts Forms* are free and guide children six through twelve around the museum. These provide direction through thought-provoking and fun questions.

On Sundays, from 12:30 to 3:30 P.M., free *Family Crafts Programs* are offered year round. *Special Children's Programs* take place during the summer. Call for times and details.

Age Range: 6 and up when using the *Gallery Adventure Sheet*. Nothing is interactive or hands-on, but if on a pre-arranged tour or with an enthusiastic parent, it will be a valuable experience. **Hours:** Tuesday, and Thursday through Saturday, 10:00 A.M. to 4:00 P.M.; Wednesday 10:00 A.M. to 8:30 P.M.; Sunday 12 noon to 4:00 P.M. Closed Mondays, July 4, Thanksgiving, Christmas, and New Year's Day. **Admission:** Free. **Time Allowance:** About an hour. **Directions:** Hyde Park. **Parking:** Metered lot on Woodlawn Avenue between 58th and 59th Streets. **Wheelchair Accessible:** Yes. **Restaurant:** No, but nearby. **Picnicking:** Yes. **Rest Rooms:** Yes, with changing tables. **Gift Shop:** Yes; rubber stamps, tote bags, jewelry.

MUSEUM OF HOLOGRAPHY
1134 West Washington Boulevard
Chicago, IL 60607
(312) 226-1007

FUN SCALE

Is it magic or science ... or maybe a little of both? Stella whips her head around, following as you pass. A pitchfork lunges at you from a bale of hay. A prisoner sways from side to side behind bars ...

Four galleries filled with state-of-the-art, 3-D laser-generated images make up the Museum of Holography. Experience mysterious laser-light images created on a light-sensitive plate by reflective patterns. The light, somehow, bounces around on other surfaces and, *viola*, instant hologram. Of course it's more complicated than this and, if you really feel the need to shatter the mystery, more-detailed explanations can be found in the museum.

The collection is extensive, consisting of holograms from North America, Europe, and Asia. Begin with the **Medical Exhibit** and experience a *lung tree*, various *bones*, and the *interior of the heart*. Step into the other gallery and see a *basket of eggs*, a *shark*, or a *dinosaur*, to name only a few.

86

Take note of the other visitors as they look at the holograms: Everyone's swaying back and forth, and bobbing up and down, trying to make the holograms react to their silliness!

Although it's a "no-touch situation," it is interactive in the sense that you create the motion through your motion. Besides, how can you touch something that's merely an illusion?

Holography One-Day Workshops are offered on Saturdays from 9:00 A.M. to 4:30 P.M. $150.00 covers the cost of tuition, lab fees, handouts, and materials. At the end of the day you can take home your own personally made hologram. It sounds great, and it is, but it's actually more for older kids, such as adults.

Age Range: 6 and up. **Hours:** Wednesday through Sunday from 12:30 to 5:00 P.M. Tour groups by appointment Monday and Tuesday. **Admission:** $2.50 7 and up. Ages 6 and under free. $3.50 with guided tour. **Time Allowance:** 30 to 45 minutes. **Directions:** West of the Loop. **Parking:** Free street. **Wheelchair Accessible:** No. **Restaurant:** No. **Picnicking:** No. **Rest Rooms:** Yes. **Gift Shop:** Yes; hologram watches, jewelry, and book marks.

GARFIELD PARK CONSERVATORY
300 North Central Park Boulevard
Chicago, IL 60624
(312) 533-1281

FUN SCALE

Take a break from the traffic and tall buildings and experience the elegance of Garfield Park Conservatory. Built in 1893, it remains one of Chicago's prominent landmarks. The four-and-one-half-acre conservatory houses an extensive collection of exotic and unusual plants and is well worth a peek.

The conservatory is broken up into diverse climatic areas containing a variety of exotic plants. **The Palm House** contains tall bamboos, Chinese fan palms, Travelers Trees, and Brazil palms. **The Aroid House** is full of colorful Bird of Paradise and sea grapes. **The Fernery** is loaded with flowerless ferns, water lilies, vanilla beans, and ginger lilies surrounded by a waterfall and pool. **The Cactus House** holds an extensive collection of plants that are acclimated to harsh climates with little water. Aside from the better known cacti, you'll see the only cactus with leaves, called Pereskia. Step inside **The Warm and Economic Houses** and you'll find an assortment of tropical plants noted for their economic value, including lemon and orange trees, cotton plants, and chewing gum trees.

Meander along the pathways through the flora, listen to the bubbling and spilling water, and smell the heavenly smells. You'll feel like you're vacationing in an exotic land. And you'll leave with a smile on your face.

Age Range: Any age. **Hours:** 9:00 A.M. to 5:00 P.M. daily. **Admission:** Free. **Time Allowance:** 30 to 60 minutes. **Directions:** Take I-290 West and exit on Independence Boulevard. Turn right on Madison Avenue and left on Central Park Boulevard. **Parking:** Free-lot. **Wheelchair Accessible:** Yes. **Restaurant:** No. **Picnicking:** Yes. **Rest Rooms:** Yes. **Gift Shop:** No.

SURVIVE ALIVE HOUSE
1010 South Clinton Street
Chicago, IL 60607
(312) 747-6691

FUN SCALE

"Fire!"

This is a horrifying cry, especially if you're not prepared. The Survive Alive House teaches, through hands-on experience, how to escape a fire.

A twelve-minute introductory video, featuring both animated and real characters, takes you step-by-step through what to do if a fire breaks out in your house. A trained fireman reviews the video, answering and asking questions. Safety steps include: having an escape plan, rolling out of bed and crawling under the smoke, and knowing two ways out of your house.

Next, step into the simulated fire in a two-bedroom house. Practice rolling off the bed and crawling under the smoke to a door or window. Climb out, go to a family meeting place, and call 911 on the mock telephone.

Afterward, ask for a free red fire helmet and junior firefighter sticker. The program is designed for groups of fifteen through thirty-five. Call ahead to see if you can join an existing group; if not, pick up the information packet and conduct a self-tour.

Across the street, at the Chicago Fire Academy, you can see where student firefighters learn how to battle modern-day flames. Be sure to check out the plaque on the lobby wall: It marks the place where the Great Fire of Chicago, which still seems to haunt the city, actually started back in 1871.

Age Range: Second through fifth graders are ideal. **Hours:** Monday through Friday 8:30 A.M. to 4:30 P.M. Closed major holidays. Call ahead for tour information. **Admission:** Free. **Time Allowance:** About an hour. **Directions:** Near West Side. **Parking:** Meter and pay-lots. **Wheelchair Accessible:** Yes. **Restaurant:** No. **Picnicking:** No. **Rest Rooms:** Yes. **Gift Shop:** No. *Cool Tip:* If your family consists of *fewer* than fifteen, call some friends and arrange for a guided tour.

THE UNITED CENTER
1901 West Madison Avenue
Chicago, IL 60612
(312) 455-4500

FUN SCALE

The United Center is home court to the Chicago Bulls and rink to the Chicago Blackhawks. It's also the site of musical concerts, ice shows, and circuses.

For a back-stage view of the center, take a guided tour. Go into the **locker rooms** and marvel at the height of the lockers and showers. Check out the suites, which are divided into three levels: **Penthouse Level**, **Club Level**, and **Lower Level**. The luxurious spaces range in price from $50,000 to $175,000 per year with a three-year contract, and contain refrigerators, TVs, and private bathrooms. (Of course, there are always the less expensive bleacher seats, but they seem miles away after you've seen the arena from the suite levels.)

At the **Press Level**, you'll see there is space for one hundred press people per event. In the **Hall of Fame Theater**, replays of Blackhawks and Bulls games flicker across a giant screen. You'll see close-up footage, lasting from fifteen to fifty-five minutes, of such greats as Scotty Pippin slam dunking into the hoop and Chris Chelios slap shotting into the goal.

Age Range: 6 and up, if a sports fan. **Hours:** Tours run on Tuesdays at 10:00 A.M. Reservations are necessary. Call for hours of events. **Admission:** Tour–Adults $5.00, seniors and children (14 and under) $3.00. **Time Allowance:** 1 1/2 hours for the tour. **Directions:** Near West Side. **Parking:** Pay-lot. **Wheelchair Accessible:** Yes. **Restaurant:** Snackbar only. **Picnicking:** No. **Rest Rooms:** Yes, with changing tables. **Gift Shop:** Yes; hockey and basketball jerseys, caps, jewelry.

BAHÁ'Í HOUSE OF WORSHIP
Wilmette, IL 60091
(708) 733-3493

FUN SCALE

What's this? A 135-foot-tall orange juice squeezer? The Bahá'í House of Worship's dome rises as if it were a mirage. No, it isn't exactly a hands-on, interactive museum laced with computers and flashing lights; but that it *is* the most visited site in the northern suburbs of Chicago gives an idea of its kid-appeal.

The eclectic mix of architectural styles in the temple reflects the Bahá'í faith. This "world religion," which originated in Persia and encompasses many Eastern influences, symbolizes the unity of all religions. Construction of the House of Worship began in 1920 and wasn't completed until 1953, which allowed a lot of time for intricate details.

Step inside and quietly experience an atmosphere of peace. Sit down and take in the breath-taking aesthetics. You'll appreciate the detailed stonework, open-domed space, and the delicate light filtering through the windows.

Outside are the formal gardens. Tulip season is a great favorite of visitors.

To get a better understanding of the Bahá'í religion, ask to see the slide presentation in the **Visitor's Center**. There's always a guide who will answer questions. To arrange for free group tours, call ahead.

Age Range: Any age with varying amounts of time. **Hours:** May 1 through September 30 from 10:00 A.M. to 10:00 P.M., daily. October 1 through April 30 from 10:00 A.M. to 5:00 P.M., daily. **Admission:** Free. **Time Allowance:** A half an hour or more. **Directions: (About 25 miles north of Chicago.)** Go north on Lake Shore Drive (Route 41) to Sheridan Road. Go through Evanston to Linden Avenue in Wilmette. **Parking:** Free-street and lot. **Wheelchair Accessible:** No, basement only. **Restaurant:** No. **Picnicking:** No, but across the street in the park. **Rest Rooms:** Yes, with changing tables. **Gift Shop:** Yes; books, pendants, cassettes.

CHICAGO BOTANIC GARDEN
Lake Cook Road
Glencoe, IL 60022-0400
(708) 835-5440

FUN SCALE

Experience three hundred acres of a living museum with exhibits that change constantly. The Chicago Botanic Garden provides a chance to see nature at its finest. Explore formal gardens, lagoons, lakes, and natural wooded areas. Grab a map before venturing out.

The **Aquatic Garden** is as good a place as any to begin your trek. In the summer you'll see water lilies galore peeking out of the water. Walk over the boardwalk that winds through the lagoon and see other water-loving plants.

The **Children's Vegetable Garden** offers disadvantaged Chicago school children a chance to try their hand at gardening during the summer months. Check out the creative scarecrows–created by the kids.

Sniff around in the splendor of the **Rose Garden**. Over five thousand rose bushes live in the garden and, on a sunny day in June, the smell is heavenly.

Another sensual delight is found in the **Sensory Garden**. Borrow the audiotape loaner at the Information Desk and listen as it takes you through the garden explaining ways other than looking to experience plants. Expand your senses and gently stroke a fuzzy Lamb's Ear. Rub and sniff the tall

fennel plants. They smell just like licorice! What color does the fruit-scented sage smell like?

Illinois once had twenty-two million acres of rolling prairie; today, only 1/10 of 1 percent is prairie land. The word for "open field" in French is *prairie* and the **Prairie** exhibit in the botanic gardens is full of nature's wild beauty, featuring Black Eyed Susans, Queen Ann's Lace, and dense brush.

Notice the bridge connecting the three **Japanese Islands** It zigzags between the second and third because the Japanese believe, if you're being followed by a demon and cross a zigzag bridge, that you'll lose him. Demons, apparently, can't zigzag!

Another option is to take the **Tram Tour**, which is narrated and winds around the grounds stopping in some of the gardens. It lasts for forty-five minutes and, although a solid overview is provided, it may be too long for squirmy kids.

Age Range: Any age. **Hours:** 7:00 A.M. to sunset daily. Closed Christmas. Tram Tours–*Mid-April through October:* weekdays 10:00 A.M. to 3:00 P.M.; weekends 10:00 A.M. to 4:00 P.M. *November through mid-April:* 11:00 A.M. to 2:00 P.M., daily. **Admission:** Free. *Tram Tour*–Adults $3.50, seniors and children (3-15) $1.75. **Time Allowance:** 2 to 4 hours. **Directions:** (25 miles north of Chicago.) Follow the Edens Expressway (I-94) north to Route 41 and exit on Lake Cook Road. Proceed east for 1/2 mile to the entrance. **Parking:** $4.00. **Wheelchair Accessible:** Yes. Free loaners available with ID. **Restaurant:** Yes, in the Education Center. **Picnicking:** Yes, in designated areas. **Rest Rooms:** Yes, with changing tables. **Gift Shop:** Yes sweatshirts, umbrellas, kid's books.

KOHL CHILDREN'S MUSEUM
165 Green Bay Road
Wilmette, IL 60091
(708) 251-7781

FUN SCALE

Here's an extremely popular place where kids play, explore, and grow. Via zillions of hands-on exhibits, kids and adults can interact and learn together. Activities are designed to encourage growth, both mental and physical.

Step on different *colored squares* and listen to the responses in many languages as you enter **People**, an exhibit aimed at breaking down prejudice and replacing it with a sense of honor. Play with a *computer* that determines the origin of your name. Another *computer* snaps a photo of you, places it on the screen, and computes the percentage of people who have the same hair color, eye color, and skin color as you. (The magnificence of modern technology!) *Paint Your Face* is a place where you can completely change your identity and act out the new one in front of a video camera. The bottom line is, we're very different on the outside but, underneath, we are all humans sharing the same planet. It's possible that through programs such as these at Kohl, kids can "nip feelings of prejudice in the bud."

Moving right along, take a **Walk Through Morocco**. Step into a traditional *Moroccan living room*. Make a *brass rubbing* and *hamsas* (good

luck symbols). Or, take a **Walk Through Jerusalem**. You can step inside a model of the walled city that lies on the other side of the world. Pull on some *native clothes* and dance a few traditional dances. Now's your chance to try bartering in the *marketplace*.

If you're an animal lover, head straight for **Kids and Pets**. Think about how it might feel being a kitty without food or a pup who desperately needs to go out for a walk. You'll learn valuable tips on how to care for your pet.

A visit to the **Dentist Office** will help familiarize kids with the often-feared setting. Role-play as a dentist or hygienist and practice brushing the *giant tooth*. Sit in the *dentist's chair* and read *x-rays* on the big screen.

For a little train action, climb on deck of **All Aboard!**, a full-scale *CTA train*. Whether you want to be the conductor or the passenger, the authentic car is there for your imagination to run wild in.

Have you ever been completely surrounded by a bubble? Or waved a wand and produced bubbles bigger than your breadbox? In full color, **Bubblemania** provides the opportunity.

Begin by making a grocery list and follow it with a hunt through the shelves of **Jewel/Osco**. Load groceries into the *shopping cart* and head for the cashier. Have you blown the budget? Have you forgotten the ice-cream? Learn all about grocery shopping.

Younger children love the **Baby Nursery**. It's a multicultural experience–the *baby dolls* are multicolored (brown, black, white, red, yellow), and the *lullabies* are sung in many languages.

Take a trip to *Where the Wild Things Are* and dress up as Max from Maurice Sendak's classic tale. Reenact the journey and stroll through the forest. Climb aboard the boat and set sail for places unknown.

Age Range: 2 to 10 years. **Hours:** Tuesday through Saturday 10:00 A.M. to 5:00 P.M. Sunday 12 noon to 5:00 P.M. Closed Monday and major holidays. **Admission:** People (1 and up) $3.00, seniors $2.50. **Time Allowance:** 1 to 2 hours. **Directions:** (About 25 miles north of Chicago.) Take the Edens Expressway (I-94) to the exit for Lake County Road and turn right on Lake-County Road. At Green Bay Road turn right. Kohl is ahead on the right. **Parking:** Free-lot. **Wheelchair Accessible:** Yes. **Restaurant:** No. **Picnicking:** No. **Rest Rooms:** Yes. **Gift Shop:** Yes; games, kids books, toys.

BELL'S ORCHARD
Route 22
Lake Zurich, IL
(708) 438-2211

FUN SCALE

Red Delicious, Macintosh, Golden Delicious, Desert Gale ... mmmn. Pick a late-summer day and head out to Bell's Orchard, one of the most popular apple orchards around. You'll find trees with branches drooping under the weight of heavy apples. It's up to you whether you pick 'em or whether you buy them pre-picked.

Take a pony ride through the grounds. Pig out at the Hog Roast in late September. Join in on occasional weekend cookouts during the months of September and October.

Age Range: Any age. **Hours:** 7:00 A.M. to 7:00 P.M. daily. Closed on some major holidays. **Admission:** *Pony rides*–$2.00, second week in September through October. **Time Allowance:** About an hour. **Directions:** (45 miles from Chicago.) Take Edens Expressway north to Half Day

Road (Route 22) and go west for 11 miles to the intersection of Route 12 (Rand Road). Continue 1/4 mile past and it's on your left. **Parking:** Free. **Wheelchair Accessible:** Mostly. **Restaurant:** Yes, lunches only, spring through fall. Call for hours. **Picnicking:** Yes, with tables and pavilion. **Rest Rooms:** Yes. **Gift Shop:** Yes; apples, pies, honey.

LAMBS FARM
P.O. Box 520
Junction I-94 and Route 176
Libertyville, IL 60048
(708) 362-4636

FUN SCALE

Lambs Farm is home to about 180 mentally retarded adults who live and work on the grounds. They learn farming and store tending, and acquire valuable life skills in the semi-private environment.

The farm provides a number of family activities and is open daily to the public. The **Farmyard** is home to *horses, rams, sheep, bunnies, donkeys, goats,* and *free-range chickens.* (Watch your step, those chickens are wild!) Most of the animals are pettable and feedable.

Step into the **Small Animal Nursery** and look at newborn animals, including *fuzzy chicks* and a *mama with baby mice.* Check out the five sleeping *ferrets.* They're snoozing because they're nocturnal–they sleep in the day and party at night. See *colorful canaries* and a *motionless boa constrictor* (in separate cages, of course). And don't miss the *adorable pot-bellied pig.*

Game of golf anyone? Tee off on the eighteen-hole **Miniature Golf Course** and test your skill against obstacles, including wooden sheep and giant stalks of corn.

Amusement rides include a **pony ride, miniature train ride,** and a trip around a **carousel**. The prices are reasonable and proceeds help support the farm.

Age Range: There's something for most ages, but children 2 to 8 will appreciate the farm most. **Hours:** *November through April*–9:00 A.M. to 3:00 P.M. daily. *May through October*–9:00 A.M. through 6:00 P.M. daily. **Admission:** *Farmyard*–Adults $1.25, children (3-13) $1.00. *Pony rides, mini-train rides,* and *fire truck rides*–All ages $1.50. *Carousel*–All ages $1.00. *Miniature golf*–All ages $2.50 per person. **Time Allowance:** 1 or 2 hours. **Directions:** Take I-294 to I-94 going north. Pass under the Wendy's Oasis and exit on Rockland Road (Route 176). Follow the signs marked by a brown lamb. **Parking:** Free. **Wheelchair Accessible:** Yes. **Restaurant:** Yes, and snackbar. **Picnicking:** Yes. **Rest Rooms:** Yes. **Gift Shop:** Yes; plastic cows, mineral jewelry, rubber snakes.

SIX FLAGS GREAT AMERICA
P.O. Box 1776
542 North Route 21
Gurnee, IL 60031
(708) 249-2133

FUN SCALE 🎈🎈🎈🎈

Anyone up for an upside-down ride, a trip to the moon, or a view of Batman in real life? If so, head to Six Flags Great America. Over two hundred acres loaded with rides, shops, eateries, and shows provide action-packed entertainment.

When most kids think of Six Flags, rides come to mind first. From heart-stopping roller coaster rides to light-hearted family rides, all levels of excitement are available. Beginning with some of the most innocuous, check out the **Columbia Carousel**. You can't miss the double-decker carousel reaching ten-stories high and consisting of about one hundred

colorful figures. If getting a little wet interests you, head to **Splashwater Falls**. The family ride takes you up a fifty-foot incline and plunges you into a lagoon of cool water below. **Roaring Rapids**, on the other hand, is less family oriented in that you're

taken on a five-minute adventure that simulates a heart-stopping, whitewater-raft expedition. Bring along a change of clothes or at least a towel. (And leave Grandma behind!)

For a beautiful high-flying view of the park, board **American Eagle.** Drop over the edge of a 147-foot hill–that's just the beginning. The double-tracked, racing wooden roller coaster is a favorite among roller coaster aficionados. For the ultimate in hair-raising experiences try **Batman The Ride**. If you're fifty-four inches or taller, and have nerves of steel, go for it! It's the first suspended, outside looping ride. (Scary!)

Have you ever thought of flying to the moon? Now's your chance. **SPACE SHUTTLE AMERICA-The Next Century** can make it happen. The multi-sensory ride simulates a journey to the moon on a five-story tall,

authentic reproduction of a NASA shuttle. Rocket through uncharted asteroid fields at heart-stopping speeds!

Live entertainment in the park ranges from musical comedy to stunt performances to cameo appearances of Warner Brother characters. **The Batman Stunt Show** is a favorite. You'll see high-action stunts performed through smoke, fire, and explosions; audience participation is required. Or head to the Theatre Royale to see **The Toonite Show**. Children up to eight years (and maybe older) will be entranced by Looney Tunes pals, including Bugs

Bunny, the Tasmanian Devil, and Daffy Duck.

The Pictorium is the place to see an **IMAX** film. Witness close-up action on the world's largest IMAX screen. Don't miss **The Six Flags Jumpin' Jammin' Jubilee Parade**. This upbeat street celebration of music, dancing, and the Looney Tune pals happens at the end of each summer day.

Age Range: Any age, but see height restrictions listed next to the rides. **Hours:** *Spring*–Saturday and Sunday; *Summer (mid-May through Labor Day)*–daily; *Fall (day after Labor Day until end of September)*–Saturday and Sunday. The Park opens at 10:00 A.M. daily. Closing times vary. **Admission:** Adults (11-59) $28.00, children (4-10) $24.00, seniors (60-plus) $14.00. 2-Day Pass $35.00. TWICKET (visit next consecutive operating day) $2.00. Pregnant women, people on crutches, or disabled pay half-price. People in wheelchairs enter for free. Pet boarding is available for approximately $3.00. **Time Allowance:** 4 hours to full-day. **Directions:** Take I-94 north to the Grand Avenue East Exit in Gurnee. Follow the signs. **Parking:** $6.00. **Wheelchair Accessible:** Yes, on most rides. Stroller and wheelchair rentals available. **Restaurant:** Yes, and snackbars. **Picnicking:** Yes. **Rest Rooms:** Yes. **Gift Shop:** Yes; T-shirts, caps, sweatshirts. *Cool Tip:* Go on July 4th, Labor Day, or Memorial Day. Believe it or not, those are the days with the *fewest* people. Otherwise, it's best to go early in the morning or late in the day. Midday gets crowded.

KIDS CONCERTS AT RAVINIA
Ravinia Festival
1575 Oakwood Avenue
Highland Park, IL 60035
(312) R-A-V-I-N-I-A

FUN SCALE

Pack up the picnic basket, find an old blanket, and head for a Kids Concert at Ravinia. Every summer Ravinia, coupled with Krafts General Foods, presents a series of kids concerts. Performances take place in a delightful, open-air 3,500-seat pavilion.

Expect to see clowns throughout the grounds performing silly, clownish pranks both before and after the kids concerts. Once the show begins, superstars of all sorts present children's music and dance in full regalia. Family favorites include jazz, swing, classical, rock, bluegrass, and folk music. Groove to the tunes of red-hot rock 'n' roll. Tap your feet to the pizzazz of jazz. From bluegrass to doo-wop, you can bop to the beat.

Performances generally promote environmental awareness, good manners and, at the very least, a sense of musical appreciation. *Viva la musica!*

Age Range: 3 to 10 for most concerts. Slightly older kids will *also* appreciate the late-summer dance concert. **Hours:** *Most* concerts take place at 11:00 A.M. on Saturdays from late June through early September. The park is open from 10:30 A.M. to 1:00 P.M. **Admission:** *Most* concerts–$5.00 for pavilion seats and $3.00 for lawn seats. **Time Allowance:** About an hour. **Directions:** (About 25 miles north of Chicago.) Take the Edens Expressway (I-94) north to the Lake-Cook Road Exit and turn right. Continue on Lake-Cook Road until Green Bay Road and turn left. Ahead on the right is Ravinia. **Parking:** Free-lot during Kids Concerts. **Wheelchair Accessible:** Yes. **Restaurant:** Snackbar only. **Picnicking:** Yes. **Rest Rooms:** Yes. **Gift Shop:** Yes; T-shirts, sweatshirts, mugs.

© Copyright Kids Concerts at Ravinia

THE POWER HOUSE

100 Shiloh Boulevard
Zion, IL 60099
(708) 746-7080

FUN SCALE

Stepping into The Power House is a little like entering a giant lightbulb. Picture a 30,000 square foot building with pipes, wiring, and ducts all exposed. The floor tiles are made of recycled lightbulbs and the picnic tables of recycled plastic. The goal of the funky design is to educate about energy in a simple, understandable, hands-on fashion.

And that's just what The Power House does. In conjunction with Commonwealth Edison, its directors have created a resource that makes learning about energy fun. (Where was it when I was growing up?) Push a button in the lobby to activate the animated introduction, then let Louis the Lightening Bug lead you through each of the museum's four main areas. Although it's not *absolutely* necessary, families can request self-guiding worksheets at the main desk.

The first section is **Nature of Energy**, and you can identify it by the color orange. Hop on the bicycle and see how much energy you need to generate 2,000 watts of power. You'll know when the light flashes!

When you're surrounded by yellow, you're in **Sources and Forms of Energy**. See a display that demonstrates how a geyser works–from the ground up. Compare gravity on different planets–pick up a liter of Pepsi on Earth, the Moon, and Jupiter. Pretend you're a pinball wizard

102

and learn about nuclear chain reactions on the Nuclear Pinball Machine. Flip the flapper and, *pfouph!*, you've created nuclear fission.

Step into the green section and you're in **Energy Use Through Time**. From water wheels in Rome to deisel generators in Chicago, the history of energy use is dramatized in interactive ways. Can you, for example, move one of the Greek columns? Tip: the more pulleys you use, the greater the weight distribution and so the less strength you have to have to do the job. Push the button to hear an explanation of what a nuclear power plant is all about. Listen, then look out the window: Across the field is a real one

In **Energy In Transition**, In the blue section, you can think about future energy sources. An energy-efficient house demonstrates examples of various conservation methods. Which do you think are most efficient? Vote for your choice on the touch computer.

Wrap your exploration up with *Energy*, a six-minute upbeat video projected on three gigantic screens.

Age Range: A majority of the exhibits are hands-on and fun for any age, conceptually; however, they're really geared for kids 8 and up. **Hours:** Monday through Saturday from 10:00 A.M. to 5:00 P.M. Closed Sunday and major holidays. **Admission:** Free. **Time Allowance:** 1 or 2 hours. **Directions:** Take I-94 North to Route 173 and proceed east toward Zion. Take a right on Sheridan Road in Zion and a left on Shiloh Boulevard (25th Street). Follow to the end and you're there. **Parking:** Free. **Wheelchair Accessible:** Yes. **Restaurant:** No, vending machines only. **Picnicking:** Yes, both inside and out. **Rest Rooms:** Yes, with changing tables. **Gift Shop:** Yes; T-shirts, science games, science books.

GARFIELD FARM MUSEUM
3No16 Garfield Road
LaFox, IL 60147
(708) 584-8485

FUN SCALE

In the 1840s you could have had a night's sleep, two meals, and shelter for your animals—and all for the price of thirty-seven and one-half cents. Of course, you may have had to share a bed with four or five strangers, but what's a little discomfort?

The farm was built by a family of ten who had moved westward from Vermont and settled on the fertile prairie land. They built an inn consisting of 80,000 hand-made bricks, grew vegetables, raised farm animals, and weathered the rough Illinois winters.

Today, visitors can explore over two hundred acres of farmland and take a tour through the restored farmhouse. Check out the bumpy beds and be sure to see the "*faux* finish" painted on some of the walls: The wood is painted with a finish to look just like a more expensive wood. (How silly!)

See goats, chickens, and two of the biggest oxen on this planet. Stroll through the heirloom gardens where herbs and veggies are grown; and try to connect yourself with the food production process. Try a hand at grinding corn or scattering the feed for chickens and geese.

Age Range: Any age. **Hours:** June through September on Wednesday and Sunday from 1:00 to 4:00 P.M. Open in other seasons, year round, from 1:00 to 4:00 P.M. by appointment. **Admission:** Donation by adults of $4.00, and children (12 and under) of $2.00, are suggested. **Time Allowance:** 1 to 2 hours. **Directions:** (40 miles west of Chicago.) From Geneva follow Illinois Route 38 West for 5 miles. Turn right and north on Garfield Road. It's 1/4 mile ahead on the left. **Parking:** Free. **Wheelchair Accessible:** Outdoor areas and first floor of the house only. **Restaurant:** No. **Picnicking:** Yes. **Rest Rooms:** Yes. **Gift Shop:** No.

© Copyright Garfield Farm Museum

GOEBBERT PUMPKIN FARM
40 West Higgins
South Barrington, IL 60010
(708) 428-6727

FUN SCALE

More than a just pumpkin farm, Goebbert's is a ride on a camel, a walk through a haunted house, and a source of scary costumes.

Changing with the seasons, Goebbert's opens in April with sales of spring planting needs. Summer brings a bounty of flowers and vegetables to the stands. When fall rolls around and cool weather sneaks in, the squashes and apples make the scene. But it's during the month of October when Goebbert's really comes to life. Loaded with pumpkins of every size, shape, and color, the farm is home to much activity.

Ghosts are your hosts and spooky music and ghoulish sounds entertain as you pass through plenty of cob webs and dark spaces in the **Haunted House**. Be prepared for minor startles, but no major heart-attack inducing scares.

Outside, wind through the maze of cut corn stalks and enter the exotic **Petting Zoo**. See *zebras, camels, emus* and other animals up-close; most are feedable and pettable. **Pony rides** happen in a ring and the **camel ride** tours the farm. You can also go for a ride on a **haywagon** that putters around the farm's thirty-some acres.

Age Range: Any age. The Haunted House is okay for both young and old. **Hours:** 9:00 A.M. to 7:00 P.M. weekdays, 9:00 A.M. to 6:00 P.M. weekends from the third week in April through Halloween Day. Haunted House open and rides available in October only. **Admission:** Haunted House $2.00; pony or camel ride $1.50; wagon rides $2.00. Petting Zoo $1.50. **Time Allowance:** About 2 hours. **Directions:** (38 miles west of Chicago.)Take I-90 West following signs for Rockford. After I-90 crosses under I-290, take Barrington Road South. At the intersection of Higgins Road (Route 72), turn right. Goebbert's is 1 mile ahead on the right. **Parking:** Free. **Wheelchair Accessible:** Yes. **Restaurant:** Cafe only; open for lunch. **Picnicking:** No. **Rest Rooms:** Yes. **Gift Shop:** Yes; scary costumes, pumpkins, fruit.

BLACKBERRY FARM
Galena Boulevard and Barnes Road
Aurora, IL 60506
(708) 892-1550

FUN SCALE

Blackberry Farm, a working nineteenth-century village, provides you with a taste of rural history.

Costumed interpreters carry out daily chores while answering your questions. Step into the **Blacksmith Shop** and see the blacksmith hammer red-hot horse shoes. Witness the environment kids learned their ABCs in the **Red Brick School House**. See wool being spun for weaving blankets and watch quilters quietly creating hand-sewn historical scenes in the **Weaver's Cabin**.

Head for **Discovery Barn** to pet and feed friendly cows, sheep, goats, pigs, and chickens. The **Farm Museum** is the place to see farm tools such as scythes and buck saws.

The **Carriage Shop Museum** houses a collection of horse-drawn vehicles that's said to be the best in the Midwest. In the **Early Streets Museum**, you'll find twelve Victorian shops.

All rides are included in the price of admission and are kid-favorites. Board the **miniature locomotive** at the Train Depot and circumnavigate

the lake. A **tractor-drawn wagon ride** follows the same route, ending at the Pioneer Cabin. Children within the height regulation (which is shorter than the board that's about four-feet high), can take a **pony ride**. The **carousel** can be ridden as many times as your heart desires!

Beautifully-kept gardens fill the fifty-five acre site, and shouldn't be missed as you tour around. Also, fishing in the lake is allowed. You must bring your own equipment, but I was told the fishing was like fishing anywhere: good if you're in luck. (Good luck!)

Age Range: Any age. **Hours:** *End of April through Labor Day*–10:00 A.M. to 4:30 P.M. daily. *Post-Labor Day through mid-October*–10:00 A.M. to 4:30 P.M., Friday, Saturday, and Sunday. **Admission:** Adults $6.00, seniors and children (2-12) $5.00. **Time Allowance:** 2 to 3 hours. **Directions:** (45 miles west of Chicago.) Take I- 290 West to I-88 West to the Orchard Road exit in Aurora. Turn left on Orchard Road and right on Galena Boulevard. Turn left on Barnes road and look for the farm on your left. **Parking:** Free-lot. **Wheelchair Accessible:** Yes. **Restaurant:** Cafeteria only. **Picnicking:** Yes, with tables. **Rest Rooms:** Yes, with changing tables in the women's rooms. **Gift Shop:** Yes; troll dolls, T-shirts, baskets.

BROOKFIELD ZOO
Chicago Zoological Park
Brookfield, IL 60513-0719
(708) 485-0263

FUN SCALE

Q: Where can you milk a goat, see penguins zip underwater, witness the world's largest bird run thirty miles per hour for up to thirty minutes, and watch polar bears swim in icy waters? A: The Brookfield Zoo.

On 215 acres the zoo houses mostly-barless, naturally-landscaped enclosures with nearly two thousand exotic and familiar animals. It was the first zoo to take animals out of cages and put them in natural habitats.

Grab a map at the gate, for there's a lot to choose from and it's easy to get disoriented. Of the twenty-four major exhibits, you might start with the **Children's Zoo**, where kids have a chance to get close-up to North American

wild and domestic animals in an enclosed environment. See chicks hatching and pet a two thousand-pound Clydesdale horse. Run your hands down the back of an armadillo, stroke a boa constrictor, or sniff a skunk. Place your hands in the touch box of *Sensory Circle*–can you guess what it is? Weather permitting, *Animal Demonstrations* take place daily.

Also, you can see how milk from a cow is turned into such foods as cheese and ice cream. Do you know that the average American eats five hundred pounds of dairy products a year? That's a lot of ice cream, even for a kid!

Safari into **Habitat Africa!**, and walk around the five-acre savanna exhibit where zebras, giraffes, and topi antelopes share the same waterhole. If you notice a baby giraffe spending the day in the shade, it's due to the fact that giraffes don't sweat and the babies, unable to store the heat in their bodies as efficiently as the mother, overheat easily. See endangered African wild dogs

roaming about on a large, rocky outcrop. Step beneath the rocky mound and see reptiles and exotic birds, and learn how they share the exceptional and limited resources of an African savanna. Check out the owls–they can't digest bones, fur, or feathers but that doesn't stop them from gobbling down their mainstay of mice and other delicacies: They throw up what won't stay down once or twice daily. (Sounds pretty gross!)

To see ocean creatures, head for the

Seven Seas Panorama. *Dolphin Shows* take place in the indoor dolphinarium seven times a day. Witness bottlenose dolphins perform spectacular stunts *or* walk down to the underwater viewing area, and watch them from below. Also in the same area is the *Seascape*, a replication of the Pacific Northwest, containing walruses, sea lions, and seals. They also can be viewed from above and below. Can you tell the difference between a sea lion and a seal? A seal has short flippers and a short neck, no external ear, and uses its back flippers to swim. A sea lion has long front flippers and a long neck, a visible ear, and uses its front flippers to swim. When swimming, sea lions look like they're flying through the water. Walruses use their tusks to dig clams, chop holes in the ice, and determine dominance among other walruses.

In the **Fragile Kingdom** you'll see the exotic worlds of both Africa and Asia. It's divided into three sections: The *Fragile Rain Forest*, an indoor Asian rain forest; the *Fragile Desert*, an indoor African desert area; and the *Fragile Hunters*, an outdoor rocky area where lions, snow leopards, jaguars, and Siberian tigers live. See how a wide variety of species depend on their environment and each other for survival.

In the **Aquatic Bird House**, you can learn about a bird's anatomy and behavior through computer games. Interact with a *flying strength machine* and test your ability to fly.

Watch exotic species such as wombats and tree kangaroos in the *Walkabout Exhibit* of the nocturnal **Australia House**. And don't miss the ibex

110

perched stately and climbing on **Ibex Island**. Now, who's king of the mountain?

For those who would rather view the zoo by tram, hop on the *Motor Safari Tour*. You're in for a forty-five minute guided tour, and you may board and reboard at your leisure. It's a nice way to get an overview.

Age Range: Any age. **Hours:** Memorial Day to Labor Day–9:30 A.M. to 5:30 P.M. daily. Labor Day to Memorial Day–10:00 A.M. to 4:30 P.M. daily. Call for dates. Children's Zoo opens at 10:00 A.M. **Admission:** *General Zoo*–Adults $4.00, seniors and children (3-11) $1.50. April through September (Tuesdays and Thursdays) admission is half-price. October through March (Tuesdays and Thursdays) admission is free. *Children's Zoo*–(plus the general zoo admission) Adults $1.00, seniors and children (3-11) $.50. *Dolphin Shows*–Adults $2.00, seniors and children (3-11) $1.50. *Motor Safari*–Adults $2.00, seniors and children $1.00. *Stroller/Wagon/Wheelchair Rentals*–Stroller $5.00 plus $5.00 deposit, wheelchairs and wagons $6.00 plus $4.00 deposit. **Time Allowance:** Full day. **Directions:** (14 miles west of Chicago.) Take I-290 West (Eisenhower Expressway). Watch for Brookfield Zoo exit signs (Exit 20), and follow First Avenue south for about 2 miles. Follow signs for the zoo. **Parking:** Cars $4.00, buses $8.00. Some free parking is available on the streets, but it's a bit of a hike. **Wheelchair Accessible:** Yes. Stroller, wheelchair, and wagon rental available. **Restaurant:** Yes, from restaurant to dairy bar. **Picnicking:** Yes, in designated picnic areas. **Rest Rooms:** Yes. **Gift Shop:** Yes; American cockroach models, giraffe socks, rubber turtles.

CANTIGNY
1 S 151 Winfield Road
Wheaton, IL 60187
(708) 668-5161

FUN SCALE

Cantigny, the five-hundred-acre estate of Colonel Robert McCormick, was named after the village in France which he, as a member of the U.S. Army's First Division, helped recapture during World War I. Due to the Colonel's proud war memories and benevolence, he established a trust fund that enabled Cantigny to open to the public in 1960. Ever since, visitors have been able to catch a piece of military history in its most colorful form.

At the **Visitor's Center**, watch the ten-minute video highlighting points of interest and giving historical background. Gather maps at the Information Area, but save the Gift Shop and Cafe for later.

Kids will want to head straight for the *tanks* outside of the First Division

Museum. From World Wars I and II, and the Korean and Viet Nam Wars, tanks decorate the lawn and are there to climb on. The **First Division Museum** is a must for most (over the age of fiveish). Military history comes to life here in an interactive manner, and is treated both heroically and in a non-glorifying manner. Pick up the *Self-guided Tour* pamphlet, and relive the battles of the First Division. Investigate farmhouses in Cantigny, traipse Omaha Beach, learn about the Cold War, meander through the jungle in Viet Nam, and watch the Operation Desert Storm video. The subject of war is delicately and sensitively handled in all these exhibits. (Kudos!)

In the **Robert McCormick Museum** you can take a guided tour of the Georgian-style mansion. Catch a glimpse of a lifestyle that no longer exists. Built in 1896 by the Colonel's grandfather, the thirty-five room estate contains collections of antiques, art work, and family mementos. The first and second floors are open to the public. The forty-five minute guided tour is a hands-off situation, but kids may appreciate strolling through such an awesome mansion. No self-guided tours are allowed.

Three miles of *trails* span across Cantigny–one, one and a half, and two and a half miles in length. They begin and end next to the tanks.

Copious gardens decorate the five hundred acres and are there for exploration; of the many, the **Idea Garden** is a favorite among kids. It includes vegetables and herbs, and has a special children's and container gardens. Learn gardening tips and plant names, but don't be fooled by the scarecrows! Check out the **Green Garden**. Did you know that so many shades of green existed? The **Rose Garden** is a must when in bloom. Take a whiff!

© Copyright Cantigny

Age Range: All ages for the gardens, 5 and up for the Military Museum, 8 and up for the McCormick Mansion tour. **Hours:** *February*–Friday through Sunday 10:00 A.M. to 4:00 P.M. *March 1 through Memorial Day*–Tuesday through Sunday 10:00 A.M. to 4:00 P.M. *Memorial Day through Labor Day*–Tuesday through Sunday 10:00 A.M. to 5:00 P.M. *Labor Day through December 29*–Tuesday through Sunday 10:00 A.M. to 4:00 P.M. Closed all of January and Mondays throughout the year. **Admission:** Free. **Time Allowance:** 2 to 4 hours. **Directions:** (25 miles west of Chicago.) I-290 West to I-88 West, exit for Naperville Road, and proceed north to Warrenville Road. Turn left on Warrenville and drive westward until Winfield Road. Turn right on Winfield and continue north for about 2 miles. Cantigny is ahead on the right. **Parking:** $3.00 per car. **Wheelchair Accessible:** Yes. Loaners available. **Restaurant:** Light snackbar only. **Picnicking:** Yes, with tables. **Rest Rooms:** Yes, with changing tables in women's rooms and some men's rooms. **Gift Shop:** Yes; bug books, plants, candles.

CERNAN EARTH AND SPACE CENTER

Triton College
2000 Fifth Avenue
River Grove, IL 60171
(708) 456-5815

FUN SCALE 🎈🎈🎈🎈

© Copyright Cernan Earth and Space Center

Take a trip to outer space and learn about our planet at the same time. Relax, lay back in the comfy chairs, and experience the mysteries of space and the puzzles of our own planet Earth. They range from Earth and Sky Shows to Children's Shows to Laser Light Shows.

Earth and Sky Shows are best for kids over eight. You're taken through volcanoes, down toboggan chutes, and up to the moon. And you never leave your seat!

Younger kids and parents will enjoy a range of **Children's Shows**. Zoom through the universe, past stars and constellations. See rocket launches and learn about other planets. Hosts include space elves and animated endangered-animal characters.

If you're up for a wild, action-packed show, you might opt for a **Laser Light Show**. Surround yourself with 360 degrees of screen, and rock out to the tunes. Multicolored laser beams combined with eardrum-blowing sound give you an exciting experience.

Weather permitting, **Monthly Skywatch** provides you with a chance to

114

see the moon, planets, and other wonders of the sky through a telescope. As the name implies, it happens just once a month.

Come back to Earth and step out into the lobby and compare the size of your foot to that of a *Brachiosaurus' print*. Look at the *"Fossils of Illinois"* collection. See the *moon gloves* and *Eugene Cernan's Apollo 10 space suit*. Cernan, after whom the center is named, walked the moon in 1972, and was the last Apollo astronaut (and the last human) to do so. Check out the shiny *RL 10-A Saturn engine*.

© Copyright Cernan Earth and Space Center

Age Range: Children's Shows are best for ages 3 through 8. Other shows for ages 8 and up.
Hours: *Earth and Sky Shows*–Thursday and Friday 7:30 P.M. Saturday several shows throughout the day. *Children's Shows*–Saturday 2:00 P.M. *Monthly Sky Watches*–some Saturdays 7:30 P.M. *Laser Light Shows*–Thursday, Friday, and Saturday evenings and nights. Call for times.
Admission: *Earth and Sky Shows, Children's Shows, or Monthly Sky Watches*–Adults $5.00, seniors and children (12 and under) $2.50. *Laser Light Shows*–Adults $5.50, seniors and children $2.75. **Time Allowance:** About an hour. **Directions:** (14 miles west of Chicago.) Take I-290 West to Exit 20. Go north on 1st Avenue, left on North Avenue, and right on 5th Avenue. Follow 5th Avenue for about 2 miles, where you'll see signs for Triton College and Cernan Center. **Parking:** Free-lot. **Wheelchair Accessible:** Yes. **Restaurant:** No. **Picnicking:** Yes. **Rest Rooms:** Yes.
Gift Shop: Yes; sunprint kits, planet holograms, globes.

FERMILAB

P.O. Box 500
Batavia, IL 60510
(708) 840-3351

FUN SCALE

© Copyright Fermilab

Picture free-range buffaloes out on a prairie, a nuclear accelerator in a basement, and 6,800 acres of open land dotted with buildings and odd shaped structures painted in brilliant yellows, oranges, and blues. Is it a scene in a science fiction movie? No, it's the setting of Fermi National Accelerator Laboratory, owned by the U.S. Department of Energy.

Fermilab, as it's commonly known, rests in a four-mile ring of land and houses the world's highest energy particle accelerator. It's considered to be an "open site," in that the accelerator is viewable and the public can visit it to gain an understanding of that mysterious force–energy.

A good starting place is **Wilson Hall**, the sixteen-story, centrally-located building. There you can gather pamphlets and hook up with a *guided tour*. However, the guided tours aren't for kids. You must be in high school or at least thirteen years old, the government states, "due to access to radiation areas." The tours go through the labs, accelerator, and main control room.

Self-guided tours, on which you *can* bring the kids, also begin in the Wilson Hall building. Pick up a tour booklet at the reception desk and set off to see videos, an accelerator model, the atrium on the first floor, the art gallery on the second floor, and exhibit areas on the

© Copyright Fermilab

fifteenth floor.

Particle probes, cosmic rays, colliding beams, and accelerator rings—yikes! Although it all may sound overwhelmingly-scientific, it's all brought down to earth in the **Lederman Science Center**. Get an idea of how physicists understand nature's secrets through twelve hands-on activities. Fool around with the *Touch Computer* and learn about electrons, protons, and particles. Place a toy car on the chute and race against accelerator paths in *Race for Energy*. Watch the "oomphmeter" light up and learn the difference between acceleration and speed. Watch waves move in the *Ripple Tank*. Step inside *Freeze a Moment in Time* and temporarily freeze your shadow on the wall. Just as quickly as it appeared, it's gone.

Children's Adventures are workshops provided by the Lederman Center, and range in length from one to twelve hours. From prairie visits to weather watching to fooling around with circles, kids are provided with hands-on, real-life experiences. Programs are offered throughout the year. Call for details.

Take a hike through the *interpretive trail* of the **restored prairie**. Don't forget to look for the buffaloes along Batavia Road. Man has traveled a long way, I thought, considering them and this place, since the days when they roamed free.

The kids won't necessarily be rocket scientists after a visit to Fermilab, but they may have learned something to dispel the mysteries of physics and, who knows, maybe you will have too!

Age Range: 2 and up for buffalo viewing and prairie walks; 5 and up for Lederman Science Center programs. **Hours:** *Lederman Science Education Center*–Monday through Friday 8:30 A.M. to 5:00 P.M., Saturday 9:00 A.M. to 3:30 P.M. *Wilson Hall*–8:30 A.M. to 5:00 P.M. daily. *Guided Tours*–Wednesday through Friday for groups of 10 or more. Call ahead for an appointment. **Admission:** General touring is free. Science Adventures vary in price. **Time Allowance:** 1 to 4 hours. **Directions:** (35 miles west of Chicago.) Take I-290 west to I-88 west and exit to Kirk Road. Travel north on Kirk Road to Pine Street. Turn east on Pine Street and enter Fermilab. The Lederman Science Center is the first building on your right and Wilson Hall is further on the right. **Parking:** Free-lots. **Wheelchair Accessible:** Yes. **Restaurant:** Cafeteria-only for lunch on weekdays. **Picnicking:** Yes. **Rest Rooms:** Yes. **Gift Shop:** Yes, in Lederman Science Center; arrowheads, magnetic marbles, tornado tubes. *Cool Tip:* Begin by heading to the fifteenth floor of Wilson Hall for an impressive view of the whole site.

THE FRANK LLOYD WRIGHT HOME AND STUDIO
951 Chicago Avenue
Oak Park, IL 60302
(708) 848-1976

FUN SCALE

© Copyright F. L. Wright Home and Studio

A kid might think that Frank Lloyd Wright is to architecture what hot fudge sauce is to an ice-cream sundae. And he wouldn't be wrong, exactly. Wright was a man of extraordinary imagination, and this is evident not only in the features of his buildings but in the thinking behind them.

You can visit the home where Wright and his family lived and the studio where he worked from 1889 to 1909. During that time, the house glistened with creativity. The house and studio exhibit remarkable features, including a balcony hung in the air by a chain harness, a skylight made of three thousand colorful pieces of glass, and a tree that grows through the wall and ceiling. The six Wright children, like their father, also were inventive and are credited with creating the original Lincoln Log structures as well as larger buildings built of other materials.

Wright was determined in all his designs to create buildings that were integrated with nature. The "Prairie" style home demonstrates his concern for both balance and imagination. In this home, you'll see the classic frieze lining the top of the walls and "tulip" pattern glass windows that look out at shingles resembling fish scales.

Be sure to check out the **Children's Playroom**, built to a child's scale. Its barrel-vaulted ceiling holds a leaf-patterned skylight and sits over a fairytale mural of a magic genie. Look up at the balcony from which playroom performances were viewed. Don't miss the grand piano that's partially built into the wall and on which Wright played Beethoven, sometimes lulling his children to sleep.

118

The **Studio** is composed of an octagonal drafting room, an office, a large reception room, and a library. You'll see more evidence here of Wright's concern for a balance with the great outdoors. High clerestory windows allow a view of nature and the sky. Stained glass windows are done in natural colors. Notice the drafting tables and try to think of the buildings that were designed on their tops: How are they in balance with nature?

A fun way for children and their parents to learn about the home and studio is to take a **Junior Tour**. These are conducted by fifth-through-eighth-grade Junior Interpreters who have been trained to point out the more kid-oriented facts. Children under eight must be accompanied by an adult. No reservations are necessary.

December brings the **Turn-of-the-Century Christmas Tour**. The free holiday tours have become a favorite tradition for many families. You'll learn how the Wrights celebrated Christmas and see the ten-foot tall Christmas tree in the children's playroom. These also are conducted by Junior Interpreters. Call for reservations and times.

Age Range: 6 and up. **Hours:** *General Tour Hours*–Monday through Friday 11:00 A.M., 1:00 P.M., and 3:00 P.M.; Saturday and Sunday 11:00 A.M. to 4:00 P.M. continuously; *Junior Tours*–Fourth Saturday of each month from January through November at 10:00 A.M. Occasional Wednesdays during the summer. *Turn-of-the-Century Christmas Tour*–First 3 Saturdays in December 9:00 to 11:00 A.M. **Admission:** *Architectural Tours*–Adult $6.00, seniors (65 and older) and youth (18 and under) $4.00. *Junior Tours*–Adults $6.00, children (6-14) $1.50. *Turn-of-the-Century Christmas Tours*–free. **Time Allowance:** About an hour. **Directions:** (10 miles west of Loop.) Take the Eisenhower Expressway (I-290) west to Harlem Avenue (Illinois 43) and exit going north. Continue on Harlem Avenue to Lake Street and turn right. Proceed until you see Oak Park ahead on your right. **Parking:** Free street and lot parking. **Wheelchair Accessible:** First floor of studio only. Video tour of house for wheelchair handicapped. Call in advance. **Restaurant:** No. **Picnicking:** Yes. **Rest Rooms:** Yes. **Gift Shop:** Yes; kid books, Wright marionettes, calendars.

© Copyright F. – Wright Home and Studio

LIZZADRO MUSEUM OF LAPIDARY ART
220 Cottage Hill, Wilder Park
Elmhurst, IL 60126
(708) 833-1616

FUN SCALE

© Copyright Lizzadro Museum of Lapidary Art

Can rocks really bend, glow in the dark, and smell like rotten eggs? In this museum you'll learn about the many foreign qualities found in rocks, and see the transformation of ordinary rocks into shiny and sometimes delicate pieces of lapidary art.

Begin with a fifteen-minute video on the history of the museum. If you're interested in a more directed self-tour, I would suggest asking for the free *scavenger hunt* at the desk. The guide, while not exactly a "hunt," presents questions for kids that will spark their interests and keep them on track.

The museum houses one of the largest collections of Chinese jade carvings in this country. See the *Nephrite Jade Boat* made about two-hundred years ago, and imagine carving out such delicate objects as the chain link attached to an anchor or the man holding a paddle.

Animal dioramas line the walls of the museum's top floor. Pick out the

120

© Copyright Lizzadro Museum of Lapidary Art

jade and jasper alligators living in the Everglades. See mice of agate chomp on cheese of jasper. Don't miss the chalcedony and Indian jasper carvings of dinosaurs. Did you know that those minerals have been around longer than dinosaurs?

If it's possible to interact with a rock, you'll do it downstairs. Find *Time Period Displays* illustrated with fossils. Push the button and hear the story of a *Gold Castle* that rests on a mountain of amethyst. Push another button and see liquid sealed inside a rock jiggle around–the agate mineral is referred to as being *"Enhydro"*. Have you ever seen a rock bend? Push the button and watch the strip of *itacolumite* curve under pressure. Activate the model train loaded with *fluorescent rocks* and watch as it travels around the tracks glowing in fluorescence.

Special programs take place on selected Saturdays. For both children and adults, they range from dinosaur videos to fossil digging. Call for more information.

© Copyright Lizzadro Museum of Lapidary Art

Age Range: 6 and up. **Hours:** Tuesday through Saturday 10:00 A.M. to 5:00 P.M., Sunday 1:00 to 5:00 P.M.; closed Monday. **Admission:** Adults $2.50, seniors (over 60) $1.50, students with IDs and teenagers $1.00, children (under 13) free. Friday is the free day. **Time Allowance:** 60 to 90 minutes. **Directions:** (16 miles west of Chicago.) Take I-290 west to Exit 14B (St. Charles Road). Go west for about 1 mile and turn right on Cottage Hill. It's 1/2 mile ahead on left. **Parking:** Free lot. **Wheelchair Accessible:** Yes. **Restaurant:** No. **Picnicking:** Yes. **Rest Rooms:** Yes. **Gift Shop:** Yes; gemstones, jewelry, books.

THE MORTON ARBORETUM
Lisle, IL 60532
(708) 719-2400

FUN SCALE

Looking for an escape from the concrete, noise, and people-overload? Then take a trip out to Lisle where the Morton Arboretum contains fifteen hundred peaceful acres planted with more than three thousand kinds of cultivated and natural vegetation from around the world–in settings ranging from intimate gardens to expansive woody areas.

On arrival, grab a map at the **Visitor Center** and see the orientation slide show. If you choose to take a **tram ride**, you'll be in for an hour-long tour around the grounds, narrated by knowledgeable guides. Be forewarned that, although the tram looks like fun for kids, an hour is an hour, and to sit in one place for that amount of time is taxing; further, the tours aren't really geared for kids.

The arboretum has twenty-five miles of walking trails, ranging from short paths through lily ponds, marshes, and meadows to long trails across woodlands and prairies. Stroll along the **Joy Path**, which passes open woodlands and perennial gardens, and leads out to **Fragrance Garden**. Take a sniff–an olfactory delight!

Or set out for a mile-long hike around **Meadow Lake** and check out the typical Illinois trees along the way. All are labeled. Hoof out to the **Prairie Trail**. Did you know that a prairie, to survive, must be completely burned every year or so in order to replenish its soil? Stroll through the very cultivated **Ground Cover Garden** surrounding the Information

Building. On a warm day, snuggle up to a good book in the **Reading Garden**.

A range of family programs are offered throughout the year such as *Parents, Tots, and Trees*; *Life in the Prairie*; *A Family Affair: Frogs and the Forest*; *Christmas Tree Ornaments*, and *Bird Watching*–to name a few. All programs range in time from one and a half hours to four days. One that shouldn't be missed is the *Family Fair* in mid-September. Experience two days of fun with discovery games, nature activities, storytelling, pumpkin painting, taffy apples, face painting, and bluegrass music. (Yee haw!)

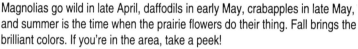

The grounds are forever changing throughout the year, of course. Magnolias go wild in late April, daffodils in early May, crabapples in late May, and summer is the time when the prairie flowers do their thing. Fall brings the brilliant colors. If you're in the area, take a peek!

Age Range: Any age. Tram Ride would be tough for squirmy kids younger than 8. **Hours:** Grounds open daily. *Daylight savings time:* 9:00 A.M. to dusk (no later than 7:00 P.M.); *Standard time:* 9:00 A.M. to 5:00 P.M. Building hours change seasonally; inquire at Visitor Center or Gatehouse. Call for tram ride times, which are irregular. **Admission:** Free. Tram Rides $2.00 per person. **Time Allowance:** 1 to 3 hours. **Directions:** (25 miles west of Chicago.) Take I-290 west to I-88 west. Exit from I-88 to Route 53, going north. It's ahead on the right. **Parking:** $6.00 per

car. Wednesdays $3.00 per car. **Wheelchair Accessible:** Yes, in buildings and on some trails. **Restaurant:** Yes, and coffee shop. **Picnicking:** Yes, in designated areas. **Rest Rooms:** Yes, with changing tables. **Gift Shop:** Yes; cool T-shirts, wind chimes, finger puppets.

SCITECH
(Science and Technology Interactive Center)
18 West Benton
Aurora, IL 60506
(708) 859-3434

FUN SCALE

In the historic post office building, site of SciTech–the Science and Technology Interactive Center—in downtown Aurora, balls bounce, bubbles pop, computers whirr, and magnets attract. Over two hundred hands-on exhibits encourage discovery and exploration in the world of science here.

Test your *bubble making* skills. Create circular patterns by using a *sand-dribbling machine*. Watch magnets make the *Chaotic Pendulum* go crazy. Experience the magic of the *Shadow Wall*. Make a *hologram* come to life. Measure your throwing speed on the *Talking Doppler* machine. (I

threw one that reached forty-eight miles per hour.) See a *hot air balloon* soar to the ceiling, then, as the air is released, gently return to the floor.

Step into **Building Blocks of the Universe** and learn about the atomic and molecular components of our physical world. Pull the arm of the *Quark Machine* and create a neutron on a computer. Play with the *Particle Smasher*, a computer game that breaks ordinary matter into its separate building blocks. Experiment with *isotopes* on a

124

computer. Look at a *Spectra* and see helium, nitrogen, and mercury in different colored gas filled tubes.

Walk downstairs, into the more intimate and less science-intimidating **KIDSPACE**. More for younger children, it's a place where they can experiment with balancing balls, vortexes, magnets, and other mystifying phenomena. Care to call someone? Use the *KidPhone*. How about becoming an anchorperson? It's your turn in the *TV News Studio*. Want to build an enormous castle? You can do it with *Soft Blocks*.

Science, like a magnet, is here to attract you!

Age Range: 2 and up. **Hours:** Wednesday, Friday, and Sunday 12 noon to 8:00 P.M.; Thursday 12 noon to 8:00 P.M.; Saturday 10:00 A.M. to 5:00 P.M. Scheduled field trips Tuesday though Friday mornings. Public welcome during field trip hours. Call for information. **Admission:** Adults (over 18) $4.00; seniors, students (under 18 with ID), and children (2-18) $2.00; family $8.00. No admission charge 5:00 to 8:00 P.M. on Thursday evenings. **Time Allowance:** About 2 hours. **Directions:** (43 miles from Chicago.) Take I-290 West to I-88 West. From I-88 exit onto Lake Street (Route 31 south) and continue until you come to Benton Street. Turn left (east) on Benton Street. SciTech is 2 blocks ahead on the right. **Parking:** Meters or metered lots. **Wheelchair Accessible:** Yes. **Restaurant:** Vending machines only. **Picnicking:** Yes. **Rest Rooms.** Yes, with changing tables. **Gift Shop:** Yes; science games, T-shirts, stickers.

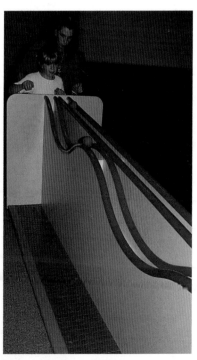

INDIANA DUNES

Indiana Dunes State Park
1600 North 25E
Chesterton, Indiana 46304
(219) 926-1952

FUN SCALE

Sand dunes so far away from the ocean? Is it a mirage?

Believe it or not, at the base of Lake Michigan, there are fifteen miles of dunes and three of them encompass sandy beaches. Having never been to the Midwest before, I was mesmerized by the sight of waves on a lake so big that you can't see to the other side and sand dunes as awesome (well, almost) as those found on Cape Cod in Massachusetts.

126

The Indiana Dunes are replete with maple and oak forests, mile upon mile of sand piles mostly covered with vegetation, marshes and bogs loaded with birds and weird flora, and easily-marked trails throughout. The vast beaches are said to be comprised of "singing sands" due to the sound caused by your tootsies as you shuffle along; in fact, the noise is a result of the friction caused by quartz crystals and moisture rubbing together.

At the **Visitor's Center**, you can pick up free maps and see a ten-minute slide show which will orient you to the dunes and amaze you with beautiful images of what you are about to see.

If you're in a bog-exploring sort of a mood, set off for **Cowles Bog**. You'll find ponds, wetlands, and marshes filled with odd plants–from delicate orchids to insect-eating Venus Fly Traps.

For a journey through time, head to **West Beach**. Hike the three-mile trail that passes through a prairie zone, a conifer zone, and an oak forest-deciduous zone, and ends on a life-guarded (summer-only) beach.

Mt Baldy is the site of the largest "living" sand dune in the National Park. It's considered to be "living" because the cottonwood trees and grasses can't take root there and, so, be held in place; the mounds of sand are active in wind and awesome anytime.

For a lo-o-o-ong stretch of white, sandy beach, head for **Kemil Beach**. Don't forget the sun screen!

Age Range: Any age. **Hours:** *Visitor Center*–(Summer) 8:00 A.M. to 6:00 P.M. daily. (Winter) 8:00 A.M. to 5:00 P.M. daily. *Beaches*–6:00 A.M. to 11:00 P.M. **Admission:** Free. **Time Allowance:** 2 hours to full day. **Directions:** (53 miles southeast of Chicago.) Take I-94 East to I-49 North (east of Porter). Follow I-94 north to Route 12. Travel east on Route 12 for 3 miles to the Dorothy Buell Memorial Visitor Center. **Parking:** Summer pay-lots and some free-lots. **Wheelchair Accessible:** Visitor's Center and some trails only. **Restaurant:** No. **Picnicking:** Yes, with barbecue pits in some areas. **Rest Rooms:** Yes. **Gift Shop:** Yes (in Visitor's Center); postcards, posters, slides.

OUTDOOR PUBLIC SCULPTURE

Why not spend a day walking from sculpture to sculpture? Downtown Chicago is loaded with fascinating outdoor public art, and the looking is free! The world-class works listed below are all within the vicinity of the Loop, and are all awesome in one form or another.

"Being Born" by Virginio Ferrari. State Street at Washington Street. Twenty-feet high and made of two shiny, stainless-steel rings, this is a climber.

"Chicago" by Joan Miró. Across from Daley Center Plaza, 69 West Washington Street. The lower periphery of this towering figure made of various media is climb-onable.

"Flamingo" by Alexander Calder. Federal Center Plaza, 210 South Dearborn Street. Made of fifty tons of bright orange steel, this stable abstract sculpture is one you can walk through and around.

"**The Four Seasons**" by Marc Chagall. First National Plaza, Monroe Street at Dearborn Street. A mosaic with more than 350 shades and hues of marble, granite, and glass, this is only for viewing. Executed in Byzantine technique, it evokes traditional imagery of Russian villages.

"**Head of a Woman**" by Pablo Picasso. Daley Civic Center Plaza, Washington Street at Dearborn Street. Known as "the Picasso," this centerpiece of the city's public art is definitely a climber and slider. The sculpture, which is the focal point of cultural gatherings and entertainment, is made of 163 tons of steel and is fifty-feet high.

"Large Interior Form" by Henry Moore. The Art Institute of Chicago, Michigan Avenue at Adams Street. A tall, curvaceous, abstract sculpture representing the human figure, this is not a climber.

"Lions" by Edward Kenneys. The Art Institute of Chicago, Michigan Avenue at Adams Street. Six thousand pounds of bronze and climb-onable. (And who can resist?)

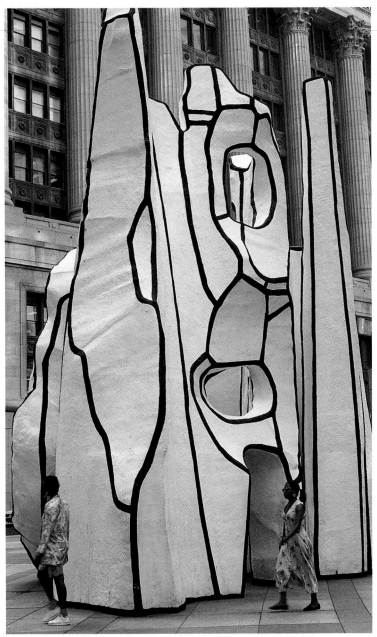

"Monument with Standing Beast" by Jean Dubuffet. James R. Thompson Center, 100 West Randolph Street. Walk through and around this massive fiberglass structure.

While observing the city's sculptures, you'll see many outdoor murals—pictures or decorations, sometimes with words and often quite large, applied directly to walls. These change, as they are by their very nature ephemeral, and sometimes the walls do too! Murals are often done anonymously and can reflect a city's temper, its vanities and flashpoints, or its triumphs and tragedies. Keep your eyes open for insight into Chicago.

CHICAGO SPORTS INFORMATION

Hear the crowd explode into thunderous applause as the team spills out onto the playing space. Feel the bleachers rumble in response to a slam-dunk, slap-shot, or home run. Live sports action is invigorating, to say the least, and sports-minded kids thrive in its charged atmosphere. Team schedules include weekend afternoon games, which are especially convenient for taking youngsters to.

Times and ticket prices vary. Call for specific information.

Baseball
Chicago Cubs
Wrigley Field
1060 West Addison Street
Chicago 60613
(312) 404-2827

Chicago White Sox
Comiskey Park
35th Street and Dan Ryan Expressway
Chicago 60616
(312) 924-1000

Basketball
Chicago Bulls
Chicago Stadium
1800 West Madison Street
Chicago 60612
(312) 943-5800

Football
Chicago Bears
Soldier Field
McFetridge Drive & Lake Shore Drive
Chicago 60605
(312) 663-5408

Hockey
Chicago Blackhawks
Chicago Stadium
1800 West Madison Street
Chicago 60612
(312) 733-5300

SPECIAL MONTHLY EVENTS

There are, of course, *many* fantastic events each month. Listed below are several of the *more* fantastic.

JANUARY

The Cultural Center offers **free films** on Tuesday nights. They're shown at 5:00 P.M. and range from foreign to documentary to popular. Some are appropriate for kids, some not. Call (312) 744-2400 for information.

Stroll through the **Lincoln Park Conservatory**. Escape the winter blues and enter a world of brilliant colors. Free admission. Call (312) 294-4770 for information.

FEBRUARY

Winter Break is sponsored by the Cultural Center and runs during winter vacation. Ice sculpture, theater, free ice skating, music, and a talent showcase are all part of the festivities. Call (312) 744-2400 for information.

The DuSable Museum of African American History celebrates **African American History Month** by offering folk songs, storytelling, games, and family crafts throughout the month. Call (312) 947-0600 for information.

MARCH

The Balzekas Museum of Lithuanian Art holds a day of **Easter Egg Decorating**. Call (312) 582-6500 for information.

APRIL

The Cultural Center celebrates the expression of dance through **Chicago Dance**, a series of dance performances and films. Call (312) 744-2400 for information.

MAY

On the first Sunday in May, about thirty businesses sponsor **Chicago Day** throughout the city. Admission is free to events including Japanese dance, choir performances, and craft demonstrations. Call (312) 744-2400 for information.

JUNE/JULY

Early June brings the **Blues Music Festival** to Grant Park. Call (312) 744-3315 for information.

Mid-June is the time for the **Gospel Music Festival** in Grant Park. Call (312) 744-3315 for more information.

The **Country Music Festival** happens late in June in Grant Park and continues through the beginning of July. Call (312) 744-3315 for more information.

Head to Grant Park for **Taste of Chicago**. From the end of June until the beginning of July, food services are open to the public with free samples of gourmet delicacies. Call (312) 744-3315 for more information.

AUGUST

The Brookfield Zoo sponsors a **Teddy Bear Picnic** during the first weekend in August. Join in the parade and teddy bear clinic. For more information call (708) 485-0263.

SEPTEMBER

Morton Arboretum sponsors **Family Day**. Call (708) 719-2400 for information.

The **Jazz Music Festival** happens early in September in Grant Park. Call (312) 744-3315 for information.

138

The **Latin Music Festival** takes place in mid-September in Grant Park. Call (312) 744-3315 for information.

OCTOBER

The Cultural Center offers a **Halloween Film Festival**. Sometimes the films are too scary for little kids. Call for (312) 744-2400 for information.

The Brookfield Zoo sponsors **Boo! At the Zoo** on the Saturday and Sunday around Halloween. Join in on the parade and costume contest. Call (708) 485-0263 for information.

Zoo Run Run takes place in mid-October on a Sunday morning. Choose between a five-kilometer race and a half-mile fun-run for kids under ten and adults with disabilities. Call (708) 485-0263 for information.

NOVEMBER

Garfield Park Conservatory holds a **Chrysanthemum Show**. Escape the early winter drabness and see a startling contrast of color. Call (312) 533-1281 for information.

DECEMBER

Join in on the **Christmas Tree Lighting Ceremony** at the Daley Civic Center Plaza. Call (312) 744-3315 for information.

The Cultural Center sponsors **"In the Spirit,"** a celebration of Hanukah, Christmas, and Kwanzaa. Festivities include a children's choir, puppets, storytelling, and films. Call (312) 477-2400 for information.

In recognition of AIDS, the Cultural Center sponsors **"Day Without Art."** Performances take place for fifteen minutes, followed by forty-five minutes of silence, and repeat throughout the day. Call (312) 477-2400 for information.

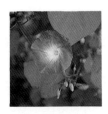

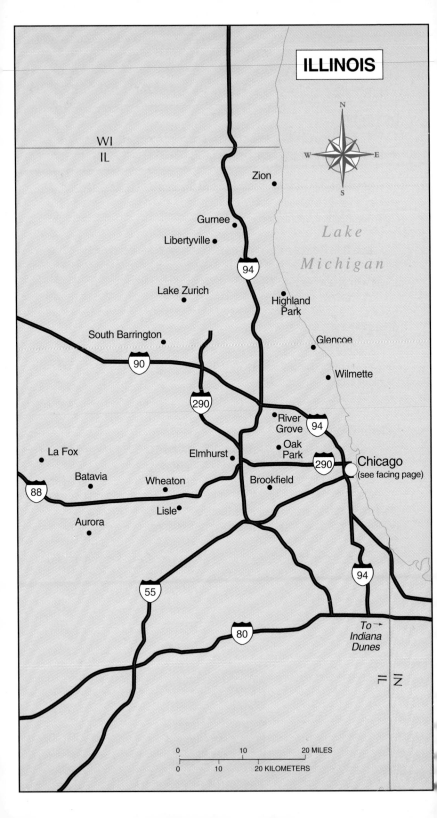

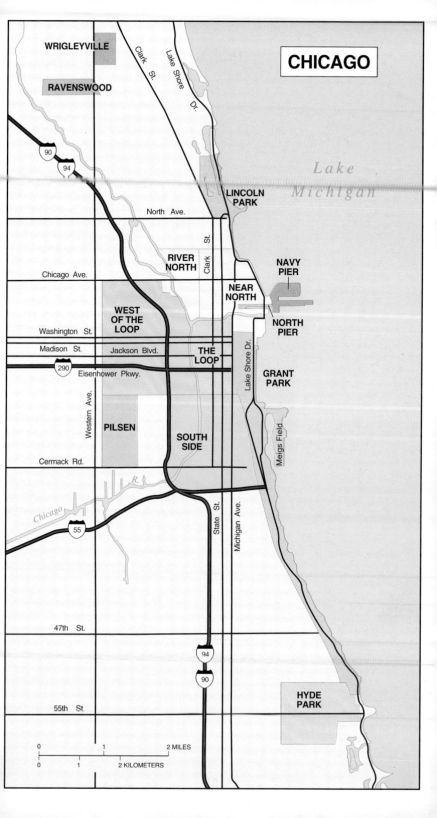

INDEX